Pancakes

Also by Dorie Greenspan

SWEET TIMES: SIMPLE DESSERTS FOR EVERY OCCASION

WAFFLES: FROM MORNING TO MIDNIGHT

BAKING WITH JULIA

Pancakes

From Morning to Midnight

. . . .

Dorie Greenspan

Quill
William Morrow
New York

It is the policy of William Morrow and Company, Inc., and its imprints and affiliates, recognizing the importance of preserving what has been written, to print the books we publish on acid-free paper, and we exert our best efforts to that end.

Library of Congress Cataloging-in-Publication Data

Greenspan, Dorie.
    Pancakes : from morning to midnight / by Dorie Greenspan.
      p.   cm.
    Includes index.
    ISBN 0-688-14104-8
    1. Pancakes, waffles, etc.   I. Title.
TX770.P34G73   1997
641.8'15—dc20   95-47353
                                                    CIP

Printed in the United States of America

First Quill Edition

1 2 3 4 5 6 7 8 9 10

BOOK DESIGN BY RENATO STANISIC

FOR JOSHUA,
THE KID I FLIP OVER DAILY

. . . .

Acknowledgments

Many thanks to the team at William Morrow, especially to my editor, Kathleen Hackett, for her insight, energy, and infectious good humor; to Harriet Bell for flipping over flapjacks at the start; to Ann Bramson and Al Marchioni for their willingness to go back to the griddle one more time; to Richard Aquan and Linda Kocur for never giving up, even when the computer did; to Judith Sutton for her always-just-so copyediting; and to Deborah Weiss Geline, the last word on words, for her intelligence, commitment, and friendship.

Thanks again to my agent, Jane Dystel, and to my "book friends," Mary Bravlove, Caroline B. Cooney, and Lorna Sass.

And, as always, my greatest thanks go to my guys, Michael and Joshua.

Contents

Flipping Through History

An Introduction to Pancakes

. . . .

First came fire, then flapjacks.

This may be a pancakecentric take on culinary history, but it's accurate. In fact, pancakes may have come before fire. Turn your imagination back and it's easy to picture an early ancestor mixing ground grains with river water, tossing the flat cakes onto a sun-heated rock, and serving up breakfast, or its prehistoric equivalent.

With roots that deep, it's no wonder pancakes became a universal food.

There isn't a culture that doesn't turn out something descended from the flapjack family tree, whether it's Russian blini, Korean battercakes, French crêpes, or Norwegian lefse.

Our own pancake tradition is long and varied. Cornmeal pancakes were a Native American staple before European settlers arrived with their versions. From the Dutch came *pannekoeken*, made with buck-wheat; from the English and French came the custom of celebrating the day before Lent, Shrove Tuesday or Mardi Gras, by binging on butter-drenched pancakes; and from America's grandest gourmet came panache: Thomas Jefferson served pancakes at Monticello.

By the early 1800s, Americans were making pancakes with white flour and calling them by names as different and descriptive as hoecakes (cooked on a field hoe, no doubt), johnnycakes (made with johnnymeal, still the name for Rhode Island cornmeal), griddle cakes, hot cakes, flat cakes, flapjacks, and flannel cakes. Indeed, the most commonly known name, pancakes, didn't make the rounds until the late nineteenth century.

After that, there was no stopping pancakes' popularity. The pancake mix that was later to become Aunt Jemima was launched in 1889 and soon restaurants began serving pancakes in assorted sizes, shapes, and flavors, none more successfully than the chain begun in 1958, the International House of Pancakes, or IHOP.

That commercially packaged and produced pancakes were "selling like hotcakes" never dampened Americans' enthusiasm for making the tasty cakes at home. Those with a passion for pancakes know that nothing compares to the aroma that floats through the kitchen when first-class pancakes come off the griddle. The fragrance alone is enough to imbue us with a feeling of well-being and of being well cared for. And that first mouthful of pancake soaked with pure maple syrup and slathered with butter is the stuff of memories, memories impossible to get from supermarket-brand frozen pancakes or pancakes from a boxed mix.

Whether you're a first timer at the griddle or a practiced hand who can send pancakes out of the skillet and into double somersaults with the flick of your wrist, the unfailing good taste, extraordinary variety, and make-a-memory power of homemade pancakes are too good to pass up.

It was with this insatiable, gotta-get-more attitude that I created the recipes for this book. Loving pancakes for breakfast, I got carried away and created "Rise-and-Shiners," the equivalent of a tall stack of new recipes, including great renditions of classics such as Cornmeal Cakes and Basic Buttermilk Pancakes, and innovative offerings like Honey-Bran Pancakes with Cheddar, Summertime Blues with Ten-Minute Blueberry Jam, Oatmeal-Raisin Pancakes with Cinnamon Sour Cream, and No-Fuss Yeast-Raised Pancakes.

But being at the griddle from morning to night inspired me to go beyond breakfast into pancakes as lunch, as a main course at dinner, as a savory side dish, and as a dessert. In the "beyond," I discovered pancakes' multiple personalities and came to understand how easily they can go from primal (Basic Pancakes) to posh (Rum-Flavored Almond Cream Crêpes are an elegant end to a dinner); from hearty (Wheat Berry Pancakes with Crunchy Salsa can be a whole meal) to ethereal (the Lemon Ricotta Hotcakes from the Four Seasons Hotel are as airy as soufflés); and from soothingly mild (Potato-Mushroom

Pancakes are the edible counterpart of a snuggle) to wake-you-up spicy (Jalapeño-Corn Cakes are jazzy).

There's a reason this food has survived for millennia. On the theory that too much of a good thing is barely enough, I offer you lots of good recipes for a very good thing, pancakes.

—DORIE GREENSPAN

Equipment for Easy Griddling

. . . .

GRIDDLES Pancakes can be made on almost any flat surface that can be heated, but as with most things culinary, the right equipment makes the job that much more pleasurable and the results that much more appealing. I created the recipes for this book using three kinds of griddles, an electric griddle, a stove-top griddle, and a cast-iron platar.

No matter what type of griddle you choose, read the instructions that come with it so you'll know how the griddle should be seasoned (most griddles, no matter the type of surface, need seasoning) and what temperature to use for making pancakes. Some electric griddles recommend a temperature of 375°F for pancakes, but I've found that with my electric griddle, 350°F is ideal. You need to play around a bit. Similarly, the instructions for my stove-top griddle suggest that medium heat is key, while I find I like to keep the heat just a tad higher.

Get to know your griddle—and don't worry, a couple of test pancakes will reveal all.

Electric griddles A good electric griddle with an easy-to-clean nonstick surface is a pancake maker's joy. The heat is even and exact, and a good griddle has a handy trough running around the edge to catch any excess butter or oil. In fact, there's an electric griddle that even has a little hole in the trough that funnels excess oil or scraped-up bits of baked pancakes into a closed container—perfect when you're using your griddle to fry bacon.

Stove-top griddles Stove-top griddles come in various sizes and finishes. My favorite is a griddle that fits across two burners (front and back) and has a nonstick surface, a run-off trough, and, as a bonus, a ridged flip side for grilling fish, meat, and vegetables.

Cast-iron platar pans A platar, similar to a Swedish pancake pan, has seven round three-inch-wide, half-inch-deep indentations for pancakes. Each round holds about two tablespoons of batter. A platar makes the neatest pancakes—each pancake is identical and cast iron, the material of choice for a platar, makes the crustiest, brownest pancakes. Cast-iron equipment is inexpensive and durable—you'll be able to pass your cast-iron pan down to future generations of pancake lovers—but it does require special care. Cast iron must be seasoned by rubbing it with oil and then heating for a few hours (follow the directions that come with your pan), and it shouldn't be scrubbed with abrasive cleansers or pads after use. The more you use cast iron, the better it gets.

SKILLETS You can use a skillet to make any of the pancakes in this book, but skillets are best reserved for sautéed pancakes, the kind that need to cook in a little oil and thus should bubble away in a pan with sides. Pull out your favorite skillet for Potato Pancakes with Applesauce like

Grandma Made or Sweet Potato–Chipotle Pancakes. And, of course, you should have a skillet ready for sautéing fruits and vegetables for toppings.

CRÊPE PAN A crêpe pan, in contrast to a skillet, has very shallow (less than an inch high) sides. Crêpe pans are usually about seven to seven and a half inches in diameter. A crêpe pan can be made of almost any metal, but I prefer one that has a nonstick surface. (Again, follow the manufacturer's directions when it comes to seasoning.) Use your crêpe pan to make sweet and savory crêpes as well as blintzes, but nothing else. You don't want to sauté in a crêpe pan (you'll scratch the surface), nor do you want to scour it and have it lose its seasoned finish.

PANCAKE TURNER Use an offset spatula or pancake flipper, one with a blade that is angled lower than the handle, to give you the maneuverability needed to get underneath and flip most pancakes. You'll want a turner with a wide blade for large pancakes and a short thin spatula, the kind used for icing, to get under pancakes and blini made in platars. If you use a griddle with a nonstick surface, check the manufacturer's instructions—you may need to use a nonmetal pancake turner to prevent nicking its surface.

HEATPROOF PLATE OR BAKING SHEET If you're not going to eat your pancakes hot off the griddle, you'll need a plate that can hold the pancakes until serving time in a 200°F oven. Alternatively, you can arrange the pancakes on a baking sheet, keep them warm in the oven, and then transfer them to a warm serving platter. Pancakes will keep for twenty minutes in a 200°F oven (see page xxxvi).

MIXING BOWLS Putting most pancake batters together requires one or two medium mixing bowls. I like to use bowls made of nonreactive materials, such as stainless steel, pottery, or glass, so I don't have to worry when mixing acidic ingredients like yogurt. It's nice to have a selection of different-sized bowls at your disposal, especially when you're making toppings for your pancakes. Look for nesting sets of stainless steel bowls in your housewares shop or supermarket—they're inexpensive and indispensable.

MEASURING CUPS AND SPOONS You should have a set of sturdy metal measuring cups and spoons for measuring dry ingredients and at least one glass measuring cup for liquid ingredients. I use two glass measuring cups—a pint measure for melting butter in the microwave oven and a quart measure for measuring the liquids in a recipe. The quart measure can double as a mixing bowl: Just add the eggs and any extracts called for in the recipe to the measured liquid and save yourself another bowl to wash.

METAL WHISK Use a medium metal whisk for combining the dry ingredients in a recipe (they just need to be stirred together, not sifted, so a whisk is the perfect tool) and for mixing the liquid ingredients into the dry.

RUBBER SPATULAS A sturdy rubber spatula is the tool of choice for scraping the last bit of batter out of a bowl and onto the griddle or for folding in ingredients. Look for commercial-grade spatulas in restaurant supply stores and housewares shops.

MICROWAVE OVEN A microwave oven is not a necessary piece of equipment for producing great pancakes, but it sure makes fast work of melting butter, heating small amounts of liquid, and cooking strips of bacon to accompany your favorite stack. Use your microwave oven as another tool in your kitchen, just don't use it to reheat pancakes—it will make them tough.

The Pancake Pantry

*A Guide to the Selection and Use of
Griddlers' Most Frequently Needed Ingredients*

BAKING POWDER Pancakes rely on double-acting baking powder for leavening. As its name suggests, double-acting baking powder works in two stages: It starts to bubble as soon as it comes into contact with the liquid ingredients in a batter, then the griddle's heat gets the second stage working. Once a tin of baking powder is opened, it's got about six months of puffing power, so replace old tins periodically.

BAKING SODA Baking soda, or bicarbonate of soda, is a component of baking powder, but it needs to be added on its own when a recipe uses acidic ingredients such as yogurt, buttermilk, or sour cream. Like baking powder, baking soda can lose its oomph; open boxes should be replenished every six months.

Broths Broth, either chicken or vegetable, is a flavorful ingredient in savory pancakes. While I use homemade broth if I have it, I always keep a supply of canned broths on hand.

Butter I use Grade AA unsalted butter in my recipes, but if you prefer salted butter, it will work just fine. Butter can be kept in the freezer for six months. Since most pancake recipes call for melted butter, you can use a heavy knife to cut off a chunk of frozen butter and return the remainder of the stick to the freezer. Whether in the refrigerator or freezer, butter should be well wrapped, since it easily picks up odors from nearby foods. While most sticks of butter come with tablespoon measurements marked on the wrappers, it's helpful to know that one 4-ounce stick of butter equals ½ cup or 8 tablespoons.

Buttermilk I love the pleasingly tart taste and tender texture that buttermilk gives to pancakes and use it frequently in my recipes. If you cannot find buttermilk in your supermarket, you can substitute a mixture of ⅔ cup plain yogurt and ⅓ cup milk for every cup of buttermilk called for in a recipe. You might be able to find powdered buttermilk in the baking supplies section of your market; follow the directions on the package to reconstitute it.

CORNMEAL For sweetness and a little crunch, cornmeal can't be beat in pancake batters. If you can find it, use stone-ground cornmeal—it will add more flavor and texture. Cornmeal, like other grain products, is best stored in the refrigerator or freezer.

DRIED FRUITS Raisins, currants, cherries, or any other dried fruits to be added to a batter should be moist and plump. (If they're hard, they won't improve on the griddle.) Shriveled, dry fruits can be rescued by covering them with boiling water and allowing them to soak for a minute, then draining them and drying them well between paper towels.

DRIED SPICES AND HERBS Dried spices and herbs should be stored in a cool dark cupboard and checked frequently for freshness—if the fragrance is gone, so is the flavor. When substituting dried spices or herbs for fresh, use half as much. When using dried leaf herbs, such as herbes de Provence or thyme, crush the leaves between your fingers to bring out their aroma before adding them to the batter.

EGGS All recipes were tested with large eggs.

EXTRACTS Like dried spices and herbs, if extracts have lost their deep, rich fragrance, you can be sure they've lost their flavor as well. Store extracts in a cool dark cupboard and check frequently. Most important, always choose extracts marked "pure"; imitation extracts won't give you true flavors.

FLOUR Most recipes in this book are made with all-purpose flour, but some call for whole wheat flour (available in supermarkets) or buckwheat flour (available in some supermarkets and most health food stores). If you don't use flour frequently, it's best to wrap it airtight and store it in the refrigerator or freezer. Before measuring flour, stir it once or twice. Then dip your metal measuring cup into the container and fill the cup to overflowing—don't pack the flour down. Take the flat side of a knife and sweep it across the measuring cup, leveling the flour but, again, not pressing down on it.

MAPLE SYRUP I can't urge you strongly enough to avoid imitation syrups, often called pancake syrup, and to use only pure maple syrup. You, your family and friends, and your pancakes deserve it. Maple syrup will keep almost indefinitely on the pantry shelf or in the refrigerator. If it clouds or crystallizes under refrigeration, just heat it by placing the opened container in a pot of barely simmering water until it clears. (Never do this with a sealed container.) This is also the best way to heat maple syrup when you want to use it as a topping for pancakes.

MILK Unless noted otherwise, you can make any of these recipes with whole, low-fat, or even skim milk. Obviously, low-fat and skim milk will give you less-rich pancakes, but fear not—they'll be delicious.

NUTS Nuts, because they're oily, can easily go rancid. Before you add nuts to a batter, it's a good idea to taste one. Unless you use nuts regularly, keep them in airtight containers in your freezer. Well wrapped, they will keep for six months. There's no need to defrost them before use.

OILS Sometimes when I'm looking for a different taste, I use oil (most often extra-virgin olive oil) instead of melted butter in a recipe. Always smell and taste your oil to make sure it's fresh before adding it to a batter. Oils should be stored in a cool, dark cupboard or the refrigerator. Refrigerated, oils will cloud, but this won't affect their taste; the clouding will clear as the oils come to room temperature.

SUGAR Granulated sugar is the sugar used most frequently in these recipes, but you'll want to have brown and confectioners' (sometimes called 10X powdered) sugars in your cupboard too. When a recipe calls for "sugar," it means granulated sugar. If it calls for "brown sugar," you can use either light or dark brown sugar. Check your brown sugar before using it to make certain it's moist and lump-free. The best way to keep brown sugar moist is to store it in airtight plastic bags.

Granulated sugar is measured by dipping the measuring cup into the canister, filling it to overflowing, and leveling it with the flat side of a knife. Confectioners' sugar should be sieved or sifted, then gently spooned into the measuring cup (if you're using only a spoonful or two, you needn't sift; just make sure there are no lumps). Brown sugar should always be firmly packed into the measuring cup or spoon by pressing the sugar into the cup or spoon with your fingers, always making sure there are no lumps (discard the lumps you can't crumble between your fingers because they won't dissolve in the batter).

VEGETABLE OIL SPRAY If your griddle needs greasing, you might want to use a vegetable oil spray. It's a quick, clean way to cover the surface lightly and evenly.

YOGURT When a recipe calls for yogurt, it means unflavored, or plain, yogurt. Feel free to use whole milk, low-fat, or even nonfat yogurt in these recipes.

Getting a Grip on Griddling
Tips for Successful Pancakes

MIX WITH A LIGHT TOUCH. There's no need to beat a pancake batter. In fact, the less mixing you do, the better. You don't want to stir up the flour's gluten, because you'll end up with tough pancakes. When mixing the liquid ingredients into the dry ingredients, stir with a whisk or rubber spatula and stop as soon as everything is combined. No need to worry about mini lumps.

GREASE THE GRIDDLE—OR DON'T. Know your griddle. If it's a nonstick model, you'll probably have to season it before you use it for the first time and then never grease it again. Ditto if you've got a well-seasoned cast-iron griddle, platar, or skillet. With any other kind of surface, you must grease each time before griddling. No matter the surface, grease it as lightly as you can using butter, oil, or a vegetable oil spray.

STEADY THE HEAT. Life is simple with an electric griddle—you just set the temperature gauge and flip away. If you're using any other kind of griddle or skillet, you'll need to find the right temperature setting. Start with medium heat and work your way up or down from there. The griddle should be hot enough so that a few drops of water sprinkled on the surface "dance" and evaporate quickly. You need this kind of heat to set the pancake batter. Once you've got the heat, you'll want to maintain—not increase—it. To familiarize yourself with your griddle, I'd suggest you make a batch of Basic Pancakes (page 2) and work out the kinks. Note what you've learned (jot it down on the page) and refer to it before starting any batch—you're bound to be successful.

POUR LOW AND SLOW. Use a ladle, pitcher, or measuring cup with a spout, or, if making small pancakes, a spoon, to pour the batter onto the griddle. Hold the ladle just two to three inches above the griddle and pour the batter slowly and evenly, keeping the ladle steady so that the batter is always being poured into the center of the pancake.

MAKE THE ROUNDS. Some pancake batters form perfect rounds as you pour them onto the griddle, others need a little nudge—the recipes will tell you which are which. If you're working with a needs-a-nudge batter, use your spatula or the back of a spoon to gently smooth the batter into a round.

SIZE THEM UP OR DOWN. You can use the same pancake batter to make silver-dollar–size cakes or pancakes big enough to put a smile on a lumberjack's face. Just vary the amount of batter you pour for the pancakes.

FLIP WITH CARE. Show off your flipping flair with sturdy flap-jacks, but delicate pancakes, lacy crêpes, and pancakes filled with chopped fruits and vegetables need tender loving care. Use a wide offset spatula with a thin blade. Gently work the flat of the spatula under as much of the pancake as you can and then, keeping close to the griddle, turn the pancake over, taking care not to let the pancake fold over on itself. If the pancakes are particularly thin, you'll need to flip with determination, using a firm hand and a quick motion to get the spatula under the cake and then using your other hand to guide the turned pancake back onto the griddle. Trust me, it sounds more complicated than it is.

KEEP THEM WARM AND TENDER. Pancakes are best hot off the griddle, but serving them as soon as they're made isn't always practical. No problem. Preheat the oven to 200°F and, as the pancakes come off the griddle, place them, slightly overlapping each other, on a heatproof platter or baking sheet; cover them loosely with a piece of foil. For extra tenderness (and goodness) brush each pancake with a little melted butter before putting it in the oven. Stacked this way, pancakes will keep for about twenty minutes, plenty of time to bake the rest of the batch.

DOUBLE THEM UP. Most pancake recipes can be multiplied directly, meaning you can double or triple the recipes without a problem. This is great if you're cooking for a crowd or want to stock your freezer. But stop at tripling the recipe—you don't want the baking powder in the mixture to lose its oomph while you're working your way through a bucketful of batter.

Readymades
Raiding the Supermarket for Toppings and Treats

While nothing beats homemade fruit syrups, chocolate sauces, or chunky jams, there are many fine pancake-perfect products to be found on supermarket shelves.

Take a tour of your market and stock your pantry, refrigerator, and freezer with treats you can use to top, fill, and serve alongside your fresh-from-the-griddle cakes. Be on the lookout for:

Unsweetened applesauce

Pure fruit spreads

Fruit butters, such as apple, apricot, and prune

Marmalades, jams, preserves, and conserves

Lemon and lime curd

Frozen berries and fruits, with or without syrup

Chocolate-hazelnut and chocolate–peanut butter spreads

Nut butters, such as cashew, almond, and peanut

Maple sugar

Pure honey, whipped, unfiltered, or in unusual flavors such as lavender or chestnut

Crème fraîche and sour cream

Soft cheeses such as Boursin and fresh goat cheese

Chutneys

Salsas

Tapenade or olivada

Tomato paste, garlic paste, and mayonnaise in tubes for savory pancakes

Griddling Ahead
Storing, Freezing, and Reheating Pancakes

Pancakes freeze and defrost perfectly, so, mix up a double batch and make some for now and some for later.

STORING: *If you're keeping pancakes for less than a day, cool them on a rack and then stack them between squares of waxed paper. Put the stacks in tightly sealed plastic bags and refrigerate until needed.*

FREEZING: *Cool pancakes to room temperature. When cool, stack them between squares of waxed paper and put them into plastic storage bags, two stacks to a bag. I've found that the best way to pack pancakes (and other baked goods) for the freezer is to press as much air out of the bag as possible and draw the top of the bag together to make a "neck"; then, to get the last bit of air out of the bag, hold the neck firmly and either insert a straw into the opening and suck out the air or simply press your lips against the opening and suck out the air. Seal the top securely with a wire twist. I double-bag everything I put in the freezer. Just put each well-sealed bag into another plastic bag and draw out the air as you did with the first one. Wrapped like this, pancakes will keep in the freezer for up to one month.*

REHEATING: *Place frozen pancakes in a single layer on a baking sheet, brush with a little melted butter (optional, but delicious), and place in a preheated 350°F oven. Frozen pancakes take ten minutes or less to heat, so it's wise to keep an eye on their progress. Alternatively, you can reheat pancakes in a toaster oven or even in the toaster; they may get a little crusty, but I know lots of people who love them that way. Avoid reheating pancakes in a microwave; they have a tendency to get soggy or rubbery, or both.*

Rise-and-Shiners

Pancakes for Breakfast

. . . .

Basic Pancakes

Pancakes 101: flapjacks for beginners—simple, fast, and foolproof. Follow the instructions and in fifteen minutes you'll have thin, perfectly round pancakes with a light inner sponge and a slightly sweet flavor you can pair with any topping.

ABOUT EIGHT 4-INCH PANCAKES

1¼ cups all-purpose flour	3 tablespoons unsalted butter, melted
2 tablespoons sugar	¼ teaspoon pure vanilla extract
1 teaspoon baking powder	
¼ teaspoon salt	
1¼ cups milk	Maple syrup, honey, or jam and butter
2 large eggs	for topping

1. In a medium bowl, whisk together the flour, sugar, baking powder, and salt. In another bowl, whisk together the milk, eggs, melted butter, and vanilla to blend thoroughly. Pour the liquid ingredients over the dry ingredients and mix with the whisk, stopping when everything is just combined. (Don't worry if the batter is a bit lumpy.)

2. If necessary, lightly butter, oil, or spray your griddle or skillet. Preheat over medium heat or, if using an electric griddle, set to 350°F. If you want to hold the pancakes until serving time, preheat your oven to 200°F.

3. Spoon ¼ cup of batter onto the griddle for each pancake, allowing space for spreading. When the undersides of the pancakes are golden and the tops are speckled with bubbles that pop and stay open, flip the pancakes over with a wide spatula and cook until the other sides are light brown. Serve immediately, or keep the finished pancakes in the preheated oven while you make the rest of the batch.

NOTE: If you want to have your own pancake mix on hand, place 5 cups flour, ½ cup sugar, 1 tablespoon plus 1 teaspoon baking powder, and 1 teaspoon salt in a large bowl. Stir with a whisk to combine, and store in a container with a tight-fitting lid. When you're ready to make a batch of pancakes, just stir the mix, measure out 1½ cups minus 2 tablespoons, and add the milk, eggs, butter, and vanilla.

SERVING: While Basic Pancakes usually get traditional toppings—butter, syrup, honey, or chunky jam—that doesn't mean you can't rustle up extras. On weekend mornings, try these with berries, yogurt, and a dusting of granola. Or consider hearty sausages, bacon, or even hot and spicy chili.

Basic Buttermilk Pancakes

Here are basic pancakes with a touch of buttermilk tartness. Buttermilk is a baker's secret weapon because, used in combination with a little baking soda, it tenderizes and adds soft, tangy undertones to a batter. In this batter, it helps produce pancakes that are light, puffy, perfectly rounded, and fluffy enough to sop up lots of good maple syrup.

ABOUT EIGHT 4-INCH PANCAKES

1 cup all-purpose flour

2 tablespoons sugar

1¼ teaspoons baking powder

¼ teaspoon baking soda

¼ teaspoon salt

1 cup buttermilk

1 large egg

3 tablespoons unsalted butter, melted

Maple syrup, honey, or jam and butter
for topping

1. In a medium bowl, whisk together the flour, sugar, baking powder, baking soda, and salt. In another bowl, whisk together the buttermilk, egg, and melted butter to blend thoroughly. Pour the liquid ingredients over the dry ingredients and mix with the whisk, stopping when everything is just combined. (Don't worry if the batter is a bit lumpy.) The batter will bubble and become spongy almost immediately.

2. If necessary, lightly butter, oil, or spray your griddle or skillet. Preheat over medium heat or, if using an electric griddle, set to 350°F. If you want to hold the pancakes until serving time, preheat your oven to 200°F.

3. Spoon ¼ cup of batter onto the griddle for each pancake, allowing space for spreading. When the undersides of the pancakes are golden and the tops are lightly speckled with bubbles that pop and stay open, flip the pancakes over with a wide spatula and cook until the other sides are light brown. Serve immediately, or keep the finished pancakes in the preheated oven while you make the rest of the batch.

S ERVING: Play these straight with butter, syrup, honey, or jam, or give them the royal treatment with poached fruits, homemade fruit butters, citrus curds, or slices of bacon. If you want to make these part of a brunch or one element in a lumberjack-style breakfast, pour out two tablespoons of batter for each pancake and you'll have silver-dollar–size cakes, just right as a side dish for hash or eggs sunny-side-up.

Cornmeal Cakes

These are the pancakes I call my house specials. They bake to a deep golden brown and have an inner sponge that's buttermilk-tender with the appealing crunch of coarsely ground cornmeal. They're a great everyday cake.

1 cup yellow cornmeal,
    preferably stone-ground
1 cup all-purpose flour
1½ teaspoons baking powder
¼ teaspoon baking soda
½ teaspoon salt
Freshly ground black pepper to
    taste (optional)

1⅔ cups buttermilk
2 large eggs
¼ cup pure maple syrup
4 tablespoons (½ stick) unsalted butter,
    melted

Maple syrup and butter for topping

1. In a medium bowl, whisk together the cornmeal, flour, baking powder, baking soda, salt, and black pepper if you're using it. In another bowl, whisk together the buttermilk, eggs, maple syrup, and melted butter to blend thoroughly. Pour the liquid ingredients over the dry ingredients and mix with the whisk, stopping when everything is just combined. (Don't worry if the batter is a bit lumpy.)

2. If necessary, lightly butter, oil, or spray your griddle or skillet. Preheat over medium heat or, if using an electric griddle, set to 350°F. If you want to hold the pancakes until serving time, preheat your oven to 200°F.

3. Spoon ¼ cup of batter onto the griddle for each pancake, allowing space for spreading. When the undersides of the pancakes are golden and the tops are speckled with bubbles that pop and stay open, flip the pancakes over with a wide spatula and cook until the other sides are light brown. Serve immediately (when these are really at their finest), or keep the finished pancakes in the preheated oven while you make the rest of the batch.

S E R V I N G :   These are a natural for sides of salty breakfast meats such as bacon, sausages, and ham steaks, and they go just as well with sweet maple syrup as with tangy cottage cheese or Crème Fraîche (page 51). In winter, try serving these with caramelized pears or spiced apple rings—the combination would be great for the-day-after-Thanksgiving breakfast.

Bacon-Cornmeal Softies

Thin, soothingly soft, bacon-salty, and cornmeal-sweet, these are the kind of pancakes you lift off the plate, roll up, and nibble as the next round bakes, only to discover you've nibbled your way through a tall stack.

ABOUT SIXTEEN 5-INCH PANCAKES

¾ cup yellow cornmeal, preferably stone-ground	2 large eggs
¾ cup all-purpose flour	⅓ cup pure maple syrup
2 teaspoons baking powder	3 tablespoons unsalted butter, melted
¼ teaspoon baking soda	5 slices bacon, cooked, drained, and diced
¼ teaspoon salt	
1¾ cups buttermilk	Maple syrup and butter for topping

1. In a medium bowl, whisk together the cornmeal, flour, baking powder, baking soda, and salt. In another bowl, whisk together the buttermilk, eggs, maple syrup, and melted butter to blend thoroughly. Pour the liquid ingredients over the dry ingredients and mix with the whisk, stopping when everything is just combined. (Don't worry if the batter is a bit lumpy.) With a rubber spatula, gently fold in the bacon bits.

2. If necessary, lightly butter, oil, or spray your griddle or skillet. Preheat over medium heat or, if using an electric griddle, set to 350°F. If you want to hold the pancakes until serving time, preheat your oven to 200°F.

3. Spoon ¼ cup of batter onto the griddle for each pancake, allowing space for spreading. When the undersides of the pancakes are golden and the tops are speckled with bubbles that pop and stay open, flip the pancakes over with a wide spatula and cook until the other sides are light brown. Serve immediately, or keep the finished pancakes in the preheated oven while you make the rest of the batch.

S ERVING : If the pancakes don't get eaten before you get them to the table, serve them as plainly and simply as you please. They're special on their own and need nothing more than maple syrup and butter to make them sublime.

Winter Buckwheat Pancakes

Of all the grains you can use to make pancakes—and you can use almost all of them—it's buckwheat that will give you cakes with the most distinctive flavor and look: a sweet, nutty taste and a deep dark brown color. These pancakes are big and puffy. I've called them winter pancakes because they're the ideal belly warmer for frosty mornings, but their flavor's a treat no matter the season.

ABOUT TWELVE 5-INCH PANCAKES

¾ cup buckwheat flour

¾ cup all-purpose flour

1½ teaspoons baking powder

½ teaspoon baking soda

½ teaspoon salt

¾ cup milk

¾ cup buttermilk

2 large eggs

4 tablespoons (½ stick) unsalted butter, melted

3 tablespoons honey

Maple syrup or honey and butter for topping

1. In a medium bowl, whisk together the buckwheat and all-purpose flours, baking powder, baking soda, and salt. In another bowl, whisk together the milk, buttermilk, eggs, melted butter, and honey to blend thoroughly. Pour the liquid ingredients over the dry ingredients and mix with the whisk, stopping when everything is just combined. (Don't worry if the batter is a bit lumpy.) You'll have a thick, dark batter that looks as though powdered coffee has been sprinkled through it; as the batter sits, it will become thicker, stickier, and more elastic—and that's fine.

10

2. If necessary, lightly butter, oil, or spray your griddle or skillet. Preheat over medium heat or, if using an electric griddle, set to 350°F. If you want to hold the pancakes until serving time, preheat your oven to 200°F.

3. Spoon ⅓ cup of batter onto the griddle for each pancake, allowing space for spreading, and use a spatula or the back of your spoon to lightly press the batter into rounds. When the undersides of the pancakes are golden and the tops are speckled with bubbles that pop and stay open, flip the pancakes over with a wide spatula and cook until the other sides are brown. Serve immediately, or keep the finished pancakes in the preheated oven while you make the rest of the batch.

SERVING: Don't play around with these. Serve them hot with just a pat of butter and some syrup or honey and let that warm buckwheat flavor shine through.

Great Grains Pancakes

I consider these pancakes the perfect please-everyone weekend brunch offering. They're light, soft, fluffy, and naturally sweet, chockful of wheat, oats, and cornmeal, and bursting with flavor. If you choose, the batter can be enriched with bacon bits, chopped apples, raisins, or nuts—or everything at once.

ABOUT FOURTEEN 4 ½ - INCH PANCAKES

¾ cup whole wheat flour	½ teaspoon salt
⅓ cup all-purpose flour	2 cups buttermilk
⅓ cup old-fashioned oats	3 large eggs
⅓ cup yellow cornmeal, preferably stone-ground	4 tablespoons (½ stick) unsalted butter, melted
2 teaspoons baking powder	¼ cup pure maple syrup
¼ teaspoon baking soda	
½ teaspoon cinnamon (optional)	Maple syrup and butter for topping

1. In a medium bowl, whisk together the whole wheat flour, all-purpose flour, oats, cornmeal, baking powder, baking soda, cinnamon if you're using it, and the salt. In another bowl, whisk together the buttermilk, eggs, melted butter, and maple syrup to blend thoroughly. Pour the liquid ingredients over the dry ingredients and mix with the whisk, stopping when everything is just combined. (Don't worry if the batter is a bit lumpy.)

2. If necessary, lightly butter, oil, or spray your griddle or skillet. Preheat over medium heat or, if using an electric griddle, set to 350°F. If you want to hold the pancakes until serving time, preheat your oven to 200°F.

3. Spoon ⅓ cup of batter onto the griddle for each pancake, allowing space for spreading. When the undersides of the pancakes are golden and the tops are speckled with bubbles that pop and stay open, flip the pancakes over with a wide spatula and cook until the other sides are light brown. Serve immediately, or keep the finished pancakes in the preheated oven while you make the rest of the batch.

SERVING: Some like these with maple syrup, others prefer Blueberry Syrup (page 35), and I think they're swell with Spiced Apple-Pear Butter (page 39). Serve them hot and take your pick.

No-Fuss Yeast-Raised Pancakes

If you've shied away from making anything with yeast, I can guarantee you success with these terrific pancakes. The yeast is dissolved, then mixed with the other ingredients, and the batter is placed in the refrigerator to rest overnight—no worrying about finding a draft-free spot or doubling in bulk. It's a snap. In fact, because the batter then needs nothing more than some eggs beaten into it in the morning, it's one of the easiest to prepare, even on weekdays. And the pancakes? They're feather-light with a yeasty, sourdough tang (it comes from the long rest period) and a chewy, bready texture that calls out for syrup.

ABOUT TWELVE 5 ½ - INCH PANCAKES

1½ cups all-purpose flour	½ cup warm water
½ cup whole wheat flour	1½ cups milk
¾ teaspoon salt	3 tablespoons unsalted butter
1 packet active dry yeast (you can use quick-rising yeast)	2 large eggs, beaten
2 tablespoons sugar	Maple syrup and butter for topping

1. In a medium bowl, whisk together the flours and salt until combined; set aside. In a large bowl, dissolve the yeast and sugar in the warm water (check the instructions on the yeast packet for the proper temperature of the water.)

2. Meanwhile, place the milk and butter in a small saucepan and heat, stirring, just until the milk is warm and the butter has melted. You don't want the milk to get any hotter than the water in which you dissolved the yeast. Working with a wooden spoon or sturdy rubber spatula, stir the milk and butter into the yeast mixture. Gradually stir the liquid ingredients into the flour mixture, mixing only until the ingredients are thoroughly combined.

3. Cover the bowl tightly with plastic wrap. You can let the batter rise at room temperature for an hour or two and then make the pancakes, or you can refrigerate the batter overnight and make the pancakes in the morning. If the batter has been refrigerated, let it rest at room temperature for 20 minutes before proceeding with the recipe.

4. When you are ready to make the pancakes, stir down the batter (it will have bubbled and risen during its rest) and then stir in the beaten eggs. You'll have a smooth, creamy batter with a wonderfully sharp, yeasty aroma.

5. If necessary, lightly butter, oil, or spray your griddle or skillet. Preheat over medium heat or, if using an electric griddle, set to 350°F. If you want to hold the pancakes until serving time, preheat your oven to 200°F.

6. Spoon ¼ cup of batter onto the griddle for each pancake, allowing space for spreading. When the undersides of the pancakes are golden and the tops are speckled with bubbles that pop and stay open, flip the pancakes over with a wide spatula and cook until the other sides are light brown. Serve immediately, or keep the finished pancakes in the preheated oven while you make the rest of the batch.

SERVING: I think one classic deserves another, so I serve these with the basics—butter and maple syrup. But I like offering sides of crisp bacon and, when I've got the time, sweetened sautéed fruits such as apples or pears.

Oatmeal-Raisin Pancakes with Cinnamon Sour Cream

Old-fashioned oats lend these raisin-dotted pancakes their nutty flavor and wonderful nubbly texture. The pancakes are puffy, thick, and only slightly sweet. Depending on the season, you might want to have bananas, berries, pears, or chunks of dried fruit stand in for the raisins.

ABOUT FOURTEEN 4-INCH PANCAKES

1 cup old-fashioned oats	4 tablespoons (½ stick) unsalted butter,
1 cup all-purpose flour	melted
¼ cup (packed) light brown sugar	½ teaspoon pure vanilla extract
2 teaspoons baking powder	1 cup plump raisins
½ teaspoon baking soda	
½ teaspoon cinnamon	
1⅔ cups buttermilk	Cinnamon Sour Cream (recipe follows)
2 large eggs	and maple syrup for topping

1. In a medium bowl, whisk together the oats, flour, brown sugar, baking powder, baking soda, and cinnamon. In another bowl, whisk together the buttermilk, eggs, melted butter, and vanilla to blend thoroughly. Pour the liquid ingredients over the dry ingredients and mix with the whisk, stopping when everything is just combined. (Don't worry if the batter is a bit lumpy.) With a rubber spatula, gently fold in the raisins. The batter will thicken as it stands.

2. If necessary, lightly butter, oil, or spray your griddle or skillet. Preheat over medium heat or, if using an electric griddle, set to 350°F. If you want to hold the pancakes until serving time, preheat your oven to 200°F.

3. Spoon ¼ cup of batter onto the griddle for each pancake, allowing space for spreading, and use a spatula or the back of your spoon to lightly press the batter into rounds. When the undersides of the pancakes are golden and the tops are speckled with bubbles that pop and stay open, flip the pancakes over with a wide spatula and cook until the other sides are light brown. Serve immediately, or keep the finished pancakes in the preheated oven while you make the rest of the batch.

Cinnamon Sour Cream

Since this topping is exceedingly simple to make, thoroughly scrumptious, and just as good over dessert pancakes as over breakfast flapjacks, you might want to whip up a double batch.

1 cup sour cream (you can use nonfat)	*1 tablespoon plus 1 teaspoon brown sugar*
	1 teaspoon cinnamon

Working in a small bowl and using a rubber spatula, thoroughly combine the ingredients. Store covered in the refrigerator until ready to serve. The cream will keep for about 1 week.

SERVING: These are best hot off the griddle—that's when they're at their puffiest. But, with Cinnamon Sour Cream and warm maple syrup, you'll enjoy them at just about any temperature. For special mornings, try these with thick-cut bacon and Buttery Bananas (page 30).

Cottage Cheese Pancakes with Cranberry Honey

Best eaten as soon as they're made, these wholesome pancakes have an outer crust that is ever so slightly crunchy and an inner sponge that is thick, soft, and custardy. Their brown sugar sweetness and cottage cheese tang make them the perfect pillows for Cranberry Honey in winter and Blueberry Syrup (page 35) in summer.

ABOUT FOURTEEN 4-INCH PANCAKES

1½ cups all-purpose flour

¼ cup (packed) light brown sugar

1½ teaspoons baking powder

¼ teaspoon baking soda

¼ teaspoon salt

1 cup cottage cheese

(you can use low-fat)

1 cup milk

2 large eggs

3 tablespoons unsalted butter, melted

½ teaspoon pure vanilla extract

Cranberry Honey (recipe follows)

for topping

1. In a medium bowl, whisk together the flour, brown sugar, baking powder, baking soda, and salt. In another bowl, whisk together the cottage cheese, milk, eggs, melted butter, and vanilla to blend thoroughly. Pour the liquid ingredients over the dry ingredients and mix with the whisk, stopping when everything is just combined. The batter will be very thick, and may be a bit lumpy.

2. If necessary, lightly butter, oil, or spray your griddle or skillet. Preheat over medium heat or, if using an electric griddle, set to 350°F. If you want to hold the pancakes until serving time, preheat your oven to 200°F.

3. Spoon ¼ cup of batter onto the griddle for each pancake, allowing space for spreading, and use a spatula or the back of your spoon to lightly press the batter into rounds. When the undersides of the pancakes are golden and the tops are speckled with bubbles that pop and stay open, flip the pancakes over with a wide spatula and cook until the other sides are light brown. Serve immediately (when these are really at their best), or keep the finished pancakes in the preheated oven while you make the rest of the batch.

continued

Cranberry Honey

What sets this topping apart is the wonderful conterpoint of cranberry's bite and honey's sweetness.

⅔ cup fresh or frozen cranberries : *¼ cup fresh orange juice*
1 cup honey :

1. Combine the cranberries, ¾ cup of the honey, and the orange juice in a medium non-reactive saucepan. Bring to a boil, lower the heat, and simmer, uncovered, for 20 minutes. The berries will pop and soften, coloring and flavoring the honey.

2. Add the remaining ¼ cup honey and simmer for another 5 minutes. Strain the honey into a jar (discarding the cranberries), cool, cover, and store in the refrigerator until ready to serve; the honey will keep for 2 weeks.

3. When you're ready to serve, warm the honey: Take the lid off the jar and place the jar in a saucepan of simmering water to come halfway up the jar. Simmer gently for a few minutes to take the chill off the honey. Alternatively, you can warm the honey by placing the open jar in a microwave oven and heating for a minute or so.

SERVING: Lovely with Cranberry Honey or a fruit syrup, Cottage Cheese Pancakes are just fine with nothing but a bit of maple syrup poured over them and slices of juicy sweet oranges served on the side.

Honey-Bran Pancakes with Cheddar

These were inspired by a muffin recipe I created for *Bon Appétit* magazine. The deeply wheaty and wonderfully cheesy flavors, bolstered with wheat bran, rounded with honey, and softened with a little vanilla, were marvelous together in muffins—and I was pleased to discover that they are equally delicious in pancakes. With the mix of grains and the cup of shredded sharp Cheddar, these are an all-in-one-breakfast; just add syrup.

ABOUT FOURTEEN 4 ½ -INCH PANCAKES

¾ cup whole wheat flour	2 large eggs
¾ cup all-purpose flour	⅓ cup honey
½ cup coarse wheat bran	3 tablespoons unsalted butter, melted
1½ teaspoons baking powder	½ teaspoon pure vanilla extract
¼ teaspoon cinnamon	1 cup shredded sharp Cheddar cheese
Pinch of nutmeg	
½ teaspoon salt	
1½ cups milk	Maple syrup for topping

1. In a medium bowl, whisk together the whole wheat and all-purpose flours, bran, baking powder, cinnamon, nutmeg, and salt. In another bowl, whisk together the milk, eggs, honey, melted butter, and vanilla to blend thoroughly. Pour the liquid ingredients over the dry ingredients and mix with the whisk, stopping when everything is just combined. (Don't worry if the batter is a bit lumpy.) With a rubber spatula, gently but thoroughly fold in the shredded cheese.

continued

21

2. If necessary, lightly butter, oil, or spray your griddle or skillet. Preheat over medium heat or, if using an electric griddle, set to 350°F. If you want to hold the pancakes until serving time, preheat your oven to 200°F.

3. Spoon ¼ cup of batter onto the griddle for each pancake, allowing space for spreading. If necessary, use a spatula or the back of your spoon to distribute the cheese evenly. When the undersides of the pancakes are quite brown and the tops are speckled with bubbles that pop and stay open, flip the pancakes over with a wide spatula and cook until the other sides are light brown. Serve immediately, or keep the finished pancakes in the preheated oven while you make the rest of the batch.

S ERVING :   Just flip these off the griddle and onto a plate, give them a gloss of syrup, and call them a great breakfast. These are so hearty that with a green salad on the side and a couple of slices of tomato on top, you could call them lunch.

Honey-Orange Pancakes with Orange Butter

Depending on what you mix with it, honey can be either sweet or pungent. Here, because it's blended with the sharp flavors of yogurt and orange, you'll taste its deeper, more pungent side. These pancakes are soft and custardy, splendid right off the griddle with pats of Orange Butter to give their tops a shine.

1¼ cups all-purpose flour

1¼ teaspoons baking powder

¼ teaspoon baking soda

⅛ teaspoon salt

1 cup plain yogurt (you can use nonfat)

½ cup fresh orange juice

1 large egg

⅓ cup honey

3 tablespoons unsalted butter, melted

⅛ teaspoon pure lemon extract

Grated zest of 1 orange

Maple syrup or honey and Orange Butter (recipe follows) for topping

1. In a medium bowl, whisk together the flour, baking powder, baking soda, and salt. In another bowl, whisk together the yogurt, orange juice, egg, honey, melted butter, and lemon extract to blend thoroughly. Pour the liquid ingredients over the dry ingredients and mix with the whisk, stopping when everything is just combined. (Don't worry if the batter is a bit lumpy.) With a rubber spatula, gently fold in the orange zest.

continued

2. If necessary, lightly butter, oil, or spray your griddle or skillet. Preheat over medium heat or, if using an electric griddle, set to 350°F. If you want to hold the pancakes until serving time, preheat your oven to 200°F.

3. Spoon ¼ cup of batter onto the griddle for each pancake, allowing space for spreading. When the undersides of the pancakes are golden and the tops are speckled with bubbles that pop and stay open, flip the pancakes over with a wide spatula and cook until the other sides are light brown. (These are soft, so you've got to get your spatula under them and flip them with conviction, or they may fold over on themselves.) Serve immediately, or keep the finished pancakes in the preheated oven while you make the rest of the batch.

Orange Butter

Orange Butter will dress up even the plainest pancakes. While you're making one batch, make two—the honey-sweetened flavored butter will keep in the freezer for at least a month.

8 tablespoons (1 stick) unsalted	*Grated zest of 2 oranges*
butter, at room temperature	*3 tablespoons honey*

Place all the ingredients in a small bowl and blend with an electric mixer or a rubber spatula until soft and creamy. Place the butter on a strip of waxed paper and form it into a log. Roll the paper up around the log, and twist the ends to seal; freeze until firm. Use the butter directly from the freezer, slicing off pats as needed, or soften in the refrigerator.

S e r v i n g : Serve Honey-Orange Pancakes hot off the griddle with a drizzle of syrup or honey and a generous slathering of Orange Butter.

Fresh Peach Pancakes with Quick Strawberry-Peach Sauce

Even stubborn sleepyheads will rouse themselves on sticky August mornings when they get a whiff of juicy summer peaches cooking in a sweet, gently spiced batter. These pancakes are laced with brown sugar, ginger, and cinnamon and shot through with chunks of fragrant peaches. They're good topped only with softened butter, but they're even more summery served with Quick Strawberry-Peach Sauce.

ABOUT FOURTEEN 4-INCH PANCAKES

1½ cups all-purpose flour

⅓ cup (packed) light brown sugar

1¼ teaspoons baking powder

¾ teaspoon ground ginger

¾ teaspoon cinnamon

1⅓ cups milk

2 large eggs

4 tablespoons (½ stick) unsalted
   butter, melted

1 tablespoon Grand Marnier or other
   orange liqueur (optional)

½ teaspoon pure vanilla extract

2 peaches, peeled, pitted, and cut into
   small dice

Quick Strawberry-Peach Sauce (recipe
   follows) or butter for topping

1. In a medium bowl, whisk together the flour, brown sugar, baking powder, ginger, and cinnamon. In another bowl, whisk together the milk, eggs, melted butter, Grand Marnier if using, and the vanilla to blend thoroughly. Pour the liquid ingredients over the dry ingredients and mix with the whisk, stopping when everything is just combined. (Don't worry if the batter is a bit lumpy.) With a rubber spatula, gently fold in the peaches.

2. If necessary, lightly butter, oil, or spray your griddle or skillet. Preheat over medium heat or, if using an electric griddle, set to 350°F. If you want to hold the pancakes until serving time, preheat your oven to 200°F.

3. Spoon ¼ cup of batter onto the griddle for each pancake, allowing space for spreading, and use a spatula or the back of your spoon to lightly press the batter into rounds. When the undersides of the pancakes are golden and the tops are speckled with bubbles that pop and stay open, flip the pancakes over with a wide spatula and cook until the other sides are light brown. Serve immediately, or keep the finished pancakes in the preheated oven while you make the rest of the batch.

Quick Strawberry-Peach Sauce

This sauce needs to be made in a blender or food processor (actually it's the perfect recipe for a hand-held, or immersion, blender), but it's so easy to make you can even put it together while you're waiting to flip your pancakes. If you have any left over, you can use it to dress up Basic Pancakes, either buttermilk (page 4) or plain (page 2).

1 cup sliced strawberries

2 peaches, peeled, pitted, and
   coarsely chopped

1 tablespoon Grand Marnier or
   other orange liqueur

¼ teaspoon pure vanilla extract

Confectioners' sugar to taste

Place the strawberries, peaches, Grand Marnier, and vanilla in a blender or a food processor fitted with the metal blade and whirl until smooth. Taste and add confectioners' sugar as needed. Store covered in the refrigerator until ready to serve; the sauce will keep for a day.

SERVING: You'll have a particularly pretty presentation if you squiggle some sauce on each plate (this is easily done if you pour the sauce into a plastic bottle with a screw-on tip, the kind often used for ketchup and mustard at diners), overlap two or three pancakes on each plate, and top with butter. If you want even more color, accompany the pancakes with some fresh berries or a spoonful of mixed fruit salad.

Banana-Pecan Pancakes with Buttery Bananas

These are substantial pancakes for hungry breakfasters. They're large and have the kind of dense inner sponge that holds on to flavors and welcomes a pat of butter and an avalanche of syrup. The combination of sweet bananas, creamy buttermilk, richly scented vanilla, and pure maple syrup makes these great for a cool-weather brunch and irresistible with the topping of Buttery Bananas.

ABOUT TWELVE 5-INCH PANCAKES

1½ cups all-purpose flour

2 tablespoons sugar

1 teaspoon baking powder

¼ teaspoon baking soda

¼ teaspoon freshly grated nutmeg

⅛ teaspoon salt

1½ cups buttermilk

2 large eggs

3 tablespoons unsalted butter,
  melted

2 tablespoons pure maple syrup

½ teaspoon pure vanilla extract

½ cup banana puree (from 1 ripe medium
  banana)

1 cup chopped pecans

Buttery Bananas (recipe follows), maple
  syrup, and toasted chopped pecans
  (optional) for topping

1. In a medium bowl, whisk together the flour, sugar, baking powder, baking soda, nutmeg, and salt. In another bowl, whisk together the buttermilk, eggs, melted butter, maple syrup, and vanilla to blend thoroughly. Pour the liquid ingredients over the dry ingredients and mix with the whisk, stopping when everything is just combined. (Don't worry if the batter is a bit lumpy.) With a rubber spatula, gently but thoroughly fold in the banana puree and chopped pecans.

2. If necessary, lightly butter, oil, or spray your griddle or skillet. Preheat over medium heat or, if using an electric griddle, set to 350°F. If you want to hold the pancakes until serving time, preheat your oven to 200°F.

3. Spoon ⅓ cup of batter onto the griddle for each pancake, allowing space for spreading. When the undersides of the pancakes are golden and the tops are speckled with bubbles that pop and stay open, flip the pancakes over with a wide spatula and cook until the other sides are light brown. Serve immediately, or keep the finished pancakes in the preheated oven while you make the rest of the batch.

continued

Buttery Bananas

Giving bananas a quick sauté in butter and brown sugar brings up their natural sweetness and lifts them above the ordinary. If you've got these on the menu for a grown-up brunch, pour three tablespoons of dark rum over the caramelized bananas while they're still in the skillet, let the rum warm, set it afire, and carefully stir the mixture until the flames subside. Spoon the bananas over the pancakes and head for the dining room.

*3 firm but ripe bananas,
thinly slicedon the diagonal*

2 teaspoons fresh lemon juice

3 tablespoons unsalted butter

2 tablespoons light brown sugar

Toss the bananas with the lemon juice. Melt the butter in a medium heavy-bottomed skillet and add the bananas. Sauté over medium heat for about 1 minute. Sprinkle the brown sugar over the bananas and continue to sauté until the sugar has melted and the bananas are lightly caramelized. Immediately remove from the heat. (The bananas can be made up to 2 hours ahead and reheated. They will be soft but lovely.)

SERVING: Arrange two or three overlapping pancakes on each plate and give them a gloss of maple syrup. Top with a few spoonfuls of the Buttery Bananas and, if you wish, a dusting of lightly toasted pecans.

Summertime Blues with Ten-Minute Blueberry Jam

When blueberries come into season, I serve them every chance I get—in waffles, muffins, fruit salads, pies, tarts, syrups (see Blueberry Syrup on page 35), and these terrific pancakes. Summertime Blues are thick, loaded with berries, tangy from yogurt and unexpectedly hearty thanks to the cornmeal. Ten-Minute Blueberry Jam makes them even better—and bluer.

ABOUT TEN 3 ½ -INCH PANCAKES

1 cup all-purpose flour

½ cup yellow cornmeal,
preferably stone-ground

¼ cup sugar

1 teaspoon baking powder

¼ teaspoon baking soda

¼ teaspoon cinnamon

¼ teaspoon salt

½ cup plain yogurt (you can
use nonfat)

½ cup milk

2 large eggs

4 tablespoons (½ stick) unsalted butter,
melted

1 teaspoon grated orange zest

¼ teaspoon pure vanilla extract

1 cup blueberries (see Note)

Ten-Minute Blueberry Jam (recipe
follows), maple syrup, and butter
for topping

1. In a medium bowl, whisk together the flour, cornmeal, sugar, baking powder, baking soda, cinnamon, and salt. In another bowl, whisk together the yogurt, milk, eggs, melted butter, orange zest, and vanilla to blend thoroughly. Pour the liquid ingredients over the dry ingredients and mix with the whisk, stopping when everything is just combined. (Don't worry if the batter is a bit lumpy.) With a rubber spatula, gently fold in the blueberries. You'll have a very thick batter resembling a muffin mixture.

2. If necessary, lightly butter, oil, or spray your griddle or skillet. Preheat over medium heat or, if using an electric griddle, set to 350°F. If you want to hold the pancakes until serving time, preheat your oven to 200°F.

3. Spoon ¼ cup of batter onto the griddle for each pancake, allowing space for spreading, and use a spatula or the back of your spoon to lightly press the batter into rounds. When the undersides are beautifully golden, flip the pancakes over with a wide spatula and cook until the other sides are light brown. (Because the pancakes are thick, they need a bit more time to bake and you may not get the normal speckling of holes.) Serve immediately, or keep the finished pancakes in the preheated oven while you make the rest of the batch.

N o t e :   If necessary, you can use frozen berries—don't thaw before adding to the batter.

Ten-Minute Blueberry Jam

This jam, which is quick, easy to make, and absolutely delicious, is bound to become a summer staple in your house. Fabulous over pancakes, it also makes a great filling for a tart.

1½ pints blueberries

3 tablespoons sugar

2 teaspoons fresh orange juice

½ teaspoon cinnamon

¼ teaspoon pure orange extract

Place 1 pint of the blueberries, the sugar, orange juice, and cinnamon in a 2-quart microwave-safe bowl or measuring cup. Stir to blend. Microwave on high, uncovered, for about 3 minutes, checking once or twice; remove from the oven when most of the berries have popped. The jam will be quite thin but it will thicken as it cools. Fold in the remaining ½ pint berries and the orange extract and let cool to room temperature. Cover and refrigerate. The jam will keep in a tightly covered jar for 2 weeks.

NOTE: If you don't have a microwave oven, you can still make fast work of the jam by simmering 1 pint of the berries, the sugar, juice, and cinnamon over medium heat until most of the berries have popped and the jam boils. Remove from the heat and add the remaining ½ cup berries and the extract.

SERVING: Go crazy—serve these plump pancakes topped with a coating of syrup and a fat pat of butter and put a dollop of Ten-Minute Blueberry Jam on the side of each plate. If you want to dress things up, edge the plates with thin slices of fresh oranges or segments of tangerines.

Morning Rice Cakes
with Blueberry Syrup

It's rare to find rice pancakes on breakfast menus nowadays and yet not so long ago they were a cookbook staple, and a delicious way to be thrifty and make good use of a bowl of leftover rice. Today, whether you use last night's rice or boil some expressly for the pancakes, you'll find these a treat—rich and filling with a nice rice "chew." You could jazz these up with spices or add fruit to the batter, but their warm, milky flavor is perfectly wonderful without fussing.

ABOUT TEN 4-INCH PANCAKES

½ cup all-purpose flour	3 tablespoons unsalted butter, melted
1 teaspoon baking powder	1½ cups cold cooked rice
2 tablespoons sugar	
¼ teaspoon freshly grated nutmeg	
¾ cup milk	Blueberry Syrup (recipe follows)
2 large eggs, separated	for topping

1. In a medium bowl, whisk together the flour, baking powder, sugar, and nutmeg. In another bowl, whisk together the milk, egg yolks, and melted butter to blend thoroughly. In a clean dry bowl, whip the egg whites with clean dry beaters until stiff but not dry. Pour the milk mixture over the flour mixture and combine with the whisk, stopping when everything is incorporated. (Don't worry if the batter is a bit lumpy.) With a rubber spatula, gently fold in the rice, then the stiffly beaten egg whites.

2. If necessary, lightly butter, oil, or spray your griddle or skillet. Preheat over medium heat or, if using an electric griddle, set to 350°F. If you want to hold the pancakes until serving time, preheat your oven to 200°F.

3. Spoon ¼ cup of batter onto the griddle for each pancake, allowing space for spreading. When the undersides of the pancakes are golden and the tops are speckled with bubbles that pop and stay open, flip the pancakes over with a wide spatula and cook until the other sides are light brown. Serve immediately, or keep the finished pancakes in the preheated oven while you make the rest of the batch.

Blueberry Syrup

I think of this as a bonus recipe, because you'll get a little more than a cup of deeply flavorful, midnight-blue syrup and a little less than a cup of cooked jammy blueberries that make a great spread. There's nothing difficult about making Blueberry Syrup, but you will need a candy thermometer.

1½ cups sugar

1 cup water

2 cups blueberries,

  at room temperature (see Note)

Grated zest of ½ lemon

4 pieces peeled fresh ginger, each the size

  of a quarter, finely minced

½ teaspoon cinnamon

Juice of ½ lemon

1. Place the sugar and water in a medium nonreactive saucepan and bring to a boil over medium-high heat, stirring with a wooden spoon until the sugar dissolves and using a brush dipped in cold water to wash down any sugar crystals that form on the sides of the pan. Reduce the heat to medium and continue to boil, without stirring, until the syrup registers 260°F on a candy thermometer.

2. Remove the pan from the heat and stir in the blueberries. Add the lemon zest, minced ginger, and cinnamon and return the pan to medium heat. Cook, stirring, for 1 minute more. Be careful! The mixture may bubble up. If necessary, work on and off heat to control bubbling. Remove the pan from the heat and add the lemon juice. Cover and let sit for an hour, or until cooled to room temperature.

3. Strain the syrup into a clean jar with a tight-fitting lid, and pack the jammy blueberries into another covered jar. Stored in the refrigerator, the syrup will keep for a month or more, the jam for about 2 weeks.

NOTE: If the blueberries are cold, they may chill the syrup so rapidly that they clump together. If this happens, work on and off heat to stir the berries into the sugar.

SERVING: Have these pancakes with Blueberry Syrup or a little maple syrup. Either way, their delicate taste shouldn't be overpowered by the addition of heavy sides like sausage. If you're serving these during the summer, you can't go wrong with a few spoonfuls of colorful berries in the center of the plate.

Apple-Walnut Pancakes with Spiced Apple-Pear Butter

All the goodness of apple pie, with flavorings subtle enough for breakfast. These pancakes feature apples two ways—grated and diced. The grated apples melt into the batter, while the diced fruit softens under the heat and sweetens the pancakes. They're great with a dollop of Spiced Apple-Pear Butter or Cinnamon Sour Cream (page 17) or just a drizzle of syrup. These are quick enough to make during the week and unusual enough for a company's-coming brunch.

ABOUT SIXTEEN 3 ½ - INCH PANCAKES

1¼ cups all-purpose flour

¼ cup (packed) brown sugar

1¼ teaspoons baking powder

¼ teaspoon baking soda

1 teaspoon cinnamon

⅛ teaspoon ground allspice

⅛ teaspoon freshly grated nutmeg

Pinch of salt

1½ cups milk

2 large eggs

4 tablespoons (½ stick) unsalted butter, melted

¾ teaspoon pure vanilla extract

2 sweet apples, peeled and cored, one cut into very fine dice and one coarsely grated

½ cup chopped walnuts

Spiced Apple-Pear Butter (recipe follows) for topping

1. In a medium bowl, whisk together the flour, brown sugar, baking powder, baking soda, cinnamon, allspice, nutmeg, and salt. In another bowl, whisk together the milk, eggs, melted butter, and vanilla to blend thoroughly. Pour the liquid ingredients over the dry ingredients and mix with the whisk, stopping when everything is just combined. (Don't worry if the batter is a bit lumpy.) With a rubber spatula, gently fold in the apples and chopped walnuts.

2. If necessary, lightly butter, oil, or spray your griddle or skillet. Preheat over medium heat or, if using an electric griddle, set to 350°F. If you want to hold the pancakes until serving time, preheat your oven to 200°F.

3. Spoon ¼ cup of batter onto the griddle for each pancake, allowing space for spreading, and use a spatula or the back of your spoon to lightly press the batter into rounds. When the undersides of the pancakes are golden and the tops are speckled with bubbles that pop and stay open, flip the pancakes over with a wide spatula and cook until the other sides are light brown. Serve immediately, or keep the finished pancakes in the preheated oven while you make the rest of the batch.

Spiced Apple-Pear Butter

It's worth making several batches of this cinnamon-accented fruit butter during the fall and winter so you're certain never to run out of it. (It will keep in the refrigerator for a month, but can be canned in a water bath for longer storage.) It's made for pancakes and is also terrific with toast, waffles, and warm pound cake.

2½ pounds cooking apples (such as Rome Beauty), peeled, cored, and coarsely chopped

2 pounds pears, peeled, cored, and coarsely chopped

1 cup apple cider or apple juice

¼ cup fresh lemon juice

½ cup granulated sugar

⅓ cup (packed) light brown sugar

1 teaspoon cinnamon

¼ teaspoon freshly grated nutmeg

One 3 × ½-inch strip orange zest

1. Position a rack in the center of your oven and preheat the oven to 350°F. Stirring, bring the apples, pears, cider, and lemon juice to a boil in a nonreactive saucepan. Reduce the heat, cover, and simmer until the fruit is tender, about 15 minutes.

2. Puree the fruit mixture in a food processor. Mix in the granulated sugar, brown sugar, cinnamon, and nutmeg. Transfer the mixture to a glass baking dish and add the zest. Bake uncovered, stirring often, until the mixture is dark and thick, 1¼ to 1½ hours. Remove the zest, transfer the fruit butter to a bowl, and cool completely.

3. Pack into an airtight container and store, refrigerated, up to 1 month.

SERVING: For special breakfasts, make these silver dollar size and serve them as an accompaniment to spicy hash, a glazed ham steak, or a bowl of steaming oatmeal.

Lemon Ricotta Hotcakes from the Four Seasons Hotel

A grand hotel breakfast is one of life's great luxuries, and few hotels are as grand as the Four Seasons in New York City. There, executive chef Susan Weaver offers breakfasts, lunches, teas, and dinners that go beyond luxury and into a megasphere of indulgence, so I was delighted when she graciously offered me this recipe from her repertoire. These "hotcakes," as she dubs them, are feathery-light, eggy, and lemony, reminiscent of a soufflé.

ABOUT TEN 3-INCH PANCAKES

3 large eggs, separated

¾ cup ricotta cheese

4 tablespoons (½ stick) unsalted
    butter, melted

½ teaspoon pure vanilla extract

¼ cup all-purpose flour

2 tablespoons sugar

Finely grated zest of 1 lemon

¼ teaspoon salt

Confectioners' sugar for topping

1. In a clean, dry medium bowl, using clean, dry beaters, whip the egg whites until they hold firm peaks; set aside. In another medium bowl, beat the ricotta, melted butter, egg yolks, and vanilla until well blended; set aside.

2. In a small bowl, whisk together the flour, sugar, lemon zest, and salt to combine. Using a rubber spatula, stir the dry ingredients into the ricotta mixture. Spoon a small amount of the beaten egg whites into the batter and mix with the rubber spatula. Gently fold in the remainder of the whites.

3. If necessary, lightly butter, oil, or spray your griddle or skillet. Preheat over medium heat or, if using an electric griddle, set to 350°F. If you want to hold the pancakes until serving time, preheat your oven to 200°F.

4. Spoon 3 tablespoons of batter onto the griddle for each pancake, allowing space for spreading. When the undersides of the pancakes are golden and the tops show a bubble or two (you won't get much, if any, speckling and popping), carefully slide a wide spatula under each pancake and gently flip them over. (The first sides of these pancakes need to cook and set a little longer than other recipes or you'll have trouble flipping them.) Cook until the other sides are light brown. Serve immediately, or keep the finished pancakes in the preheated oven while you make the rest of the batch.

SERVING: Chef Weaver suggests dusting the pancakes with confectioners' sugar and garnishing the plate with berries. They're wonderful that way, but they can also take maple syrup or homemade Blueberry Syrup (page 35), and Thick Lemon Curd (page 94) makes them food fit for a celebration.

2

Beyond Breakfast

Savory Cakes for Noon and Night

. . . .

Potato Pancakes with Applesauce like Grandma Made

As soon as the first potato pancake hits the oil, I am transported to my grandmother's kitchen. Her potato pancakes never made it to the dining room—everyone would hang around the stove and grab them the instant she put them on brown paper to drain. No one seemed to care about burned fingers. My mother used to call these "knuckle cakes" because inevitably my grandmother would skin a knuckle or three grating the potatoes on her battered box grater. Knuckles are not a vital ingredient in these tasty cakes, and food processors make the grating a cinch. The outsides of these pancakes are crispy and brown, like the famous Swiss potato dish rösti, and the insides are soft and pale. It's almost as though they were made from two different vegetables.

ABOUT TWELVE 3-INCH PANCAKES

2 russet potatoes (total weight about 1 pound), peeled

¼ medium onion

2 tablespoons all-purpose flour

1 large egg

1 teaspoon salt

½ teaspoon freshly ground black pepper

Peanut oil for sautéing

Homemade Applesauce (recipe follows) or sour cream for topping

1. Using the large holes of a box grater or the grating blade of a food processor, grate the potatoes and onion, and place them in a bowl.

2. In a medium bowl, whisk together the flour, egg, salt, and pepper. Pick up a small amount of the potatoes and onions and press it between the palms of your hands to extract as much of the liquid as possible. Add the pressed mixture to the flour mixture and continue until you've worked your way through all the potatoes and onions. This sounds messier and more time-consuming than it really is; you can do it all in about 3 minutes. Stir the mixture to blend.

3. These should be eaten as close as possible to the time they emerge from the skillet; however, if you need to keep the pancakes for a short time before serving, preheat your oven to 200°F. Pour enough peanut oil to come ⅛ inch up the sides of a large cast-iron or other heavy skillet and heat over medium heat until the oil is very hot but not bubbling—a little piece of potato put into the oil should start frying immediately. While the oil is heating, line a baking sheet with a brown paper bag or a triple thickness of paper towels.

4. For each pancake, lift about 2 tablespoons of batter out of the bowl with a slotted spoon (you want to avoid the accumulated liquid) and carefully place the batter in the hot oil. Press the cake down with the back of the spoon to create a thin pancake 2½ to 3 inches across. Be careful not to crowd the pan—leave about 2 inches of space between the pancakes. Cook the pancakes until they are deep brown and crispy on the undersides, then turn with a wide spatula and a fork and brown the other sides; the total cooking time is about 8 minutes. Lift the pancakes out of the oil, letting the excess oil drip back into the skillet, and place on the brown paper to drain. Pat the tops of the pancakes free of excess oil with paper toweling and serve immediately, or keep, uncovered, in the warm oven while you make the rest of the batch.

continued

Homemade Applesauce

Good old-fashioned unsweetened applesauce like this is remarkably easy to make at home, and batch after batch can be delightfully different, depending on the apples you choose.

3 large apples : *3 tablespoons water*

1. Cut the apples into eighths and put the pieces, seeds, core, peel, and all, in a heavy-bottomed pan (see Note). Add the water and bring to a simmer over medium-low heat. Cover the pan and cook, stirring occasionally, until the apples fall apart when pressed, about 20 minutes. If the apples can be mashed into a sauce but if there's too much liquid in the pan, uncover and cook for another 5 minutes, stirring all the while.
2. Pass the sauce through a food mill with a medium blade. If the sauce looks thin, return it to the pan and cook away the excess liquid, stirring constantly. Serve warm, at room temperature, or chilled. Refrigerated, the sauce will keep for 1 to 2 weeks.

NOTE: If you do not have a food mill, peel and core the apples before cooking them. Cook until the apples are soft enough to beat into a sauce with a wooden spoon. If you want a smoother sauce, pass it through a strainer.

SERVING: When I was growing up, these were served with sour cream or applesauce, but in my own home I've been known to dress them to the nines with Crème Fraîche (page 51), paper-thin slices of silky smoked salmon, and snipped fresh chives, and to serve them with flutes of Champagne. Not many foods go from plain to fancy so deliciously.

Herbed Potato Pancakes

I made the first batch of these sparkling-green sautéed potato pancakes when my herb garden was just starting to come into its own, and then continued to make them all summer long with varying combinations of fresh-clipped herbs, including parsley, rosemary, and thyme as well as basil and chives. If you don't have an herb garden or access to a variety of fresh herbs, or if you want to make these during the winter, they're fine with just parsley or a mix of parsley and watercress.

ABOUT FIFTEEN 2½-INCH PANCAKES

2 russet potatoes (total weight about 1 pound), peeled and cut into chunks

1 medium onion, peeled

½ cup (packed) fresh herbs, minced

2 large eggs

1¼ teaspoons salt

1 teaspoon freshly ground black pepper

¼ cup all-purpose flour

Peanut oil for sautéing

Glistening Parsley Drizzle (page 75) for topping

1. Place the potatoes, onion, and herbs in a food processor fitted with the metal blade and process until pureed. Add the eggs, salt, and pepper and process until well blended. Sprinkle over the flour and pulse just until it is incorporated. Transfer the batter to a medium bowl.

continued

2. If you want to keep the pancakes for a short time before serving, preheat your oven to 200°F. Pour enough peanut oil to come ⅛ inch up the sides of a large cast-iron or other heavy skillet and heat over medium heat until the oil is very hot but not bubbling. While the oil is heating, line a baking sheet with a brown paper bag or a triple thickness of paper towels.

3. For each pancake, lift about 2 tablespoons of batter out of the bowl with a slotted spoon (you want to avoid the accumulated liquid) and carefully place the batter in the hot oil. Press the cake down with the back of the spoon to create a thin pancake about 2½ inches across. Be careful not to crowd the pan—leave about 2 inches of space between the pancakes. Cook the pancakes until they are golden on the undersides, then turn with a wide spatula and a fork and brown the other sides. Lift the pancakes out of the oil, letting the excess oil drip back into the skillet, and place on the brown paper to drain. Pat the tops of the pancakes free of excess oil with paper toweling and serve immediately (when they're best), or keep in the warm oven while you make the rest of the batch.

S ERVING : These are good plain and great with a little Glistening Parsley Drizzle (page 75) or just a spoonful of sour cream or Crème Fraîche (page 51). Turn to these when you're searching for the right companion for your favorite fish dish or you're looking for an out-of-the-ordinary go-along for a platter of grilled vegetables and a bowl of mixed greens.

Potato-Mushroom Pancakes with Crème Fraîche

These start with great mashed potatoes mixed with leeks and mushrooms. Cooked through on the griddle, their interior remains as soft, satisfying, and comforting as the spuds of childhood while the outsides develop a light, delicate, and golden crust. The final gloss of porcini oil (available in specialty shops) is a fragrant luxury and a nice touch with the tang of homemade crème fraîche.

ABOUT EIGHTEEN 3-INCH PANCAKES

2 russet potatoes (total weight about 1 pound), peeled and cut into small pieces

2 tablespoons unsalted butter

1 medium leek, white part only, washed, dried, and very thinly sliced

3 large mushroom caps, cleaned and cut into very small dice

1 teaspoon herbes de Provence or ½ teaspoon dried thyme

Salt and freshly ground black pepper to taste

¾ cup heavy cream

2 large eggs

3 tablespoons all-purpose flour

1 teaspoon baking powder

Porcini oil and Crème Fraîche (recipe follows) or sour cream for topping

continued

1. Boil or steam the potatoes until they can be pierced easily with a fork. Drain well and turn into a large bowl. Mash the potatoes using a potato ricer or the back of a large serving spoon. Mix in 1 tablespoon of the butter.

2. Melt the remaining tablespoon of butter in a large sauté pan. Add the leek and mushrooms and sauté until the leek is softened and the mushrooms are nicely browned. Add the vegetables, with any cooking juices, to the potatoes and mix well. Add the herbes de Provence, and season generously with salt and pepper.

3. Whisk the heavy cream and eggs together in a small bowl, and add to the potato mixture, beating until thoroughly combined. In another small bowl, whisk together the flour and baking powder. Use a rubber spatula to fold the flour into the potatoes.

4. If necessary, lightly butter, oil, or spray your griddle or skillet. Preheat over medium heat or, if using an electric griddle, set to 350°F. If you want to hold the pancakes until serving time, preheat your oven to 200°F.

5. Spoon 3 tablespoons of batter onto the griddle for each pancake, allowing space for spreading, and use a spatula or the back of your spoon to lightly press the batter into rounds. When the undersides of the pancakes are golden (you won't get much bubbling on the tops of these pancakes), carefully slide a wide spatula under each pancake and turn gently, taking care that it doesn't fold over on itself. Cook until the other sides are light brown. As soon as the pancakes come off the griddle, brush them lightly with porcini oil. Serve immediately, or keep the finished pancakes in the preheated oven while you make the rest of the batch.

Crème Fraîche

Crème fraîche is sour cream's French cousin. However, unlike sour cream, crème fraîche can be whipped into peaks or heated without separating. These days, crème fraîche is often available in the dairy sections of supermarkets, but it's much more expensive than the tart crème fraîche you can make easily at home. Just remember, you need to start making the crème at least a day before you want to use it. Crème fraîche is wonderful in place of sour cream over savory pancakes, and it can be sweetened to be used with breakfast and dessert pancakes.

1 cup heavy cream   *2 tablespoons buttermilk*

1. Place the cream and buttermilk in a clean jar with a lid. Cover the jar and shake vigorously to mix. Allow the jar to stand at room temperature until the cream thickens a bit; this can take 8 to 12 hours, or longer if your room is quite cold.

2. When thickened, place in the refrigerator to chill. The crème fraîche can be kept for about 3 weeks in the refrigerator. It will get tarter and tangier the longer it is stored.

SERVING: These make a super side dish to chicken dishes, roasts, and simply grilled fish. Serve them with just a brush of porcini oil and crème fraîche or sour cream. If you want to make a really big deal of these, serve them as a first course, brushed with porcini oil, topped with a little crème fraîche and an abundance of sautéed wild mushrooms, and placed on a bed of lightly dressed mixed greens.

Sweet Potato–Chipotle Pancakes

Be warned: Anyone with a taste for things hot and spicy will find these addictive. These are among my all-time favorite pancakes. They've got the comforting, soft insides and crispy, sautéed outsides of Potato Pancakes with Applesauce like Grandma Made (page 44), plus the smoke and fire of chili powder and chipotle peppers. (Chipotles are smoked jalapeño peppers and they're available canned, packed in a spicy sauce called adobo, in specialty markets and some supermarkets.)

You can serve these with a sour cream topping as a buffet or before-dinner nibble, but I have a feeling that you'll have the same experience with these that my grandmother had with her potato pancakes—they'll never get out of the kitchen. I've made these many times and the scene has always been the same: The smell of sautéing sweet potatoes draws people into the kitchen and the next thing you know, they're gobbling down pancakes as they come out of the skillet.

ABOUT SIXTEEN 2 ½ -INCH PANCAKES

1 pound sweet potatoes, peeled	1½ teaspoons salt
3 canned chipotle peppers, pureed	Peanut oil for sautéing
1 large egg, beaten	
1 tablespoon honey	
½ cup all-purpose flour	Sour cream or Crème Fraîche (page 51)
1¾ teaspoons chili powder	for topping

1. Grate the sweet potatoes using the grating blade of a food processor or the large holes of a box grater. Transfer the grated potatoes to a medium bowl and add the chipotles, egg, and honey. Stir with a rubber spatula to combine the ingredients.

2. In a small bowl, whisk together the flour, chili powder, and salt. Add the dry ingredients to the potato mixture and stir with the spatula just until incorporated.

3. If you want to keep the pancakes for a short time before serving, preheat your oven to 200°F. Pour enough peanut oil to come ⅛ inch up the sides of a large cast-iron or other heavy skillet and heat over medium heat until the oil is very hot but not bubbling. While the oil is heating, line a baking sheet with a brown paper bag or a triple thickness of paper towels.

4. For each pancake, drop a rounded tablespoon of batter into the oil and press the cake down with the back of the spoon to create a thin pancake that's about 2½ inches across. Be careful not to crowd the pan—leave about 2 inches of space between the pancakes. Cook the pancakes until they are deep brown and crispy on the undersides, then turn with a wide spatula and a fork and brown the other sides. Lift the pancakes out of the oil, letting the excess oil drip back into the skillet, and place on the brown paper to drain. Pat the tops of the pancakes free of excess oil with paper toweling and serve immediately, or keep, uncovered, in the warm oven while you make the rest of the batch.

SERVING: You could serve these as a side dish to chicken, pot roast, or a meaty fish like tuna or swordfish, but I think they are best served on their own as an appetizer or nibble with drinks before dinner or during a cocktail party. Top each pancake with sour cream or crème fraîche and serve with plenty of cold beer or chilled fruity white wine.

Zucchini Baby Cakes

Oniony, garlicky, golden, and green, these small pancakes retain the crunch and flavor of garden-fresh zucchini because the raw vegetable is grated into the pancake batter and cooks for just minutes on the griddle. I like these really spicy, so I go heavy on the black pepper. I also like these plain, without a topping, served alongside fish cooked on the grill.

ABOUT TWELVE 2 ½-INCH PANCAKES

1 medium zucchini	½ teaspoon freshly ground black pepper
¼ medium onion	1 tablespoon olive oil
2 cloves garlic, pressed	1 large egg, beaten
¼ teaspoon freshly grated nutmeg	¼ cup all-purpose flour
¾ teaspoon salt	½ teaspoon baking powder

1. Grate the zucchini and onion, using the large holes of a box grater or the grating blade of a food processor. Place the zucchini and onion in a large bowl; you should have about 2 packed cups. Stir in the garlic, nutmeg, salt, pepper, olive oil, and beaten egg. In a small bowl, whisk together the flour and baking powder. Fold the dry ingredients into the zucchini mixture with a rubber spatula. You'll have a very loose, liquidy mixture.
2. If necessary, lightly butter, oil, or spray your griddle or skillet. Preheat over medium heat or, if using an electric griddle, set to 350°F. If you want to hold the pancakes until serving time, preheat your oven to 200°F.

3. Because this batter is so wet, make certain your griddle is the right temperature when you start—you want the batter to set the instant it hits the griddle. Spoon 3 tablespoons of batter onto the griddle for each pancake, making sure you get both liquid and solids (at the end, you may have some liquid left over), and allowing space for spreading. Use a spatula or the back of your spoon to lightly press the batter into rounds. The shapes will be irregular. When the undersides of these delicate pancakes are golden, (you won't get much bubbling on the tops of these pancakes), flip the pancakes over with a wide spatula and cook until the other sides are light brown. Serve immediately, or keep the finished pancakes in the preheated oven while you make the rest of the batch.

S E R V I N G : These are just fine served plain as a side dish or as the "bread" for a salad lunch. If you want to top them, think about a thick slice of juicy tomato, a dab of Easy Aïoli (page 61), or a sheet of shaved Parmesan cheese.

Wheat Berry Pancakes with Crunchy Salsa

Wheat berries are the whole grain of wheat with just the husk removed. When you scoop them out of the bin at your local health food market, their look, a cross between pale wild rice and dark barley, won't give you a clue as to how delicious and satisfying they'll be after they're soaked and boiled. They take time to prepare, but they're worth it. And they're uncommonly good in these pancakes, which have a lot of crunch and chew.

ABOUT TWELVE 4-INCH PANCAKES

1 tablespoon plus 2 teaspoons olive oil	½ teaspoon salt
2 shallots, minced	¼ teaspoon freshly ground black pepper
2 scallions, white part only, very thinly sliced	1 cup vegetable or chicken broth
1 small onion, minced	2 large eggs
1 clove garlic, minced	1 tablespoon soy sauce
1 cup all-purpose flour	¼ teaspoon Tabasco sauce
¾ teaspoon baking powder	¼ teaspoon Asian sesame oil
1 teaspoon herbes de Provence or ¼ teaspoon dried thyme	1 cup cooked wheat berries (see Note)
	Crunchy Salsa (recipe follows) for topping

1. In a small skillet, heat 2 teaspoons of the olive oil over medium heat. Add the shallots, scallions, onion, and garlic and sauté until softened, 3 to 5 minutes; cool.

2. In a medium bowl, whisk together the flour, baking powder, herbs, salt, and pepper. In another bowl, whisk together the broth, eggs, soy sauce, Tabasco, sesame oil, and the remaining tablespoon of olive oil. Pour the liquid ingredients over the dry ingredients and mix with the whisk, stopping when everything is combined. You'll have a very liquid batter. With a rubber spatula, gently fold in the wheat berries.

3. If necessary, lightly butter, oil, or spray your griddle or skillet. Preheat over medium heat or, if using an electric griddle, set to 350°F. If you want to hold the pancakes until serving time, preheat your oven to 200°F.

4. Spoon ¼ cup of batter onto the griddle for each pancake, making sure to get both wheat berries and liquid and leaving ample space for spreading. When the undersides of the pancakes are pale golden (they won't get very brown), flip the pancakes over with a wide spatula and cook until the other sides are light brown. Serve immediately, or keep the finished pancakes in the preheated oven while you make the rest of the batch.

N O T E :   Wheat berries double in volume when cooked, so ½ cup of raw berries will yield 1 cup of cooked. However, I suggest that you cook more than you'll need for this recipe and use the leftovers in salads or stuffings, or as a side dish.

In a medium saucepan, cover the raw wheat berries with cold water and soak for 5 hours, or overnight. Partially cover the saucepan and cook the wheat berries in their soaking liquid for 50 to 60 minutes, until softened, adding more water if necessary. Drain and let cool. Cooked wheat berries will keep well covered in the refrigerator for about 3 days.

continued

Crunchy Salsa

This is the kind of salsa I often make in large quantity, using some to top Wheat Berry Pancakes and the leftovers as the centerpiece of a light supper. There's nothing sacred about the combination of ingredients or the amount of each ingredient. Use what you've got on hand and what you like most; just try to keep the ingredients colorful and cut them into small pieces of fairly uniform size—the rest is up for grabs.

2 teaspoons white wine vinegar, or
  more to taste
¼ teaspoon Dijon mustard
¼ teaspoon herbes de Provence
Salt and freshly ground black pepper
  to taste
1½ tablespoons extra-virgin olive oil,
  or more to taste
½ red bell pepper, cored, seeded,
  deveined, and diced

½ medium cucumber, peeled, seeded, and
  diced
½ apple, cored but unpeeled, diced
½ cup corn kernels, fresh, frozen (thawed),
  or canned (drained)
2 scallions, white part only, minced
2 tablespoons plump currants or raisins

In a medium bowl, whisk together the wine vinegar, mustard, herbes de Provence, and salt and pepper. Slowly add the oil, whisking all the while, until smooth and emulsified. Taste and correct the seasonings, adding more vinegar or oil if desired. Add the remaining ingredients and toss to coat the fruits and vegetables with dressing. Cover and chill until ready to serve. You can make the salsa a few hours ahead and keep it refrigerated.

SERVING: Topped with Crunchy Salsa, these can be lunch. If you've got some Easy Aïoli (page 61), spread a little over each pancake before dressing with the salsa. Without the salsa, the pancakes are ideal with a stew or roast; just moisten with a little cooking juice.

Roasted Garlic Pesto Pancakes with Easy Aïoli

Pesto is one of the most popular sauces ever to be stirred into pasta. Traditionally, it's a shimmering blend of basil, garlic, olive oil, Parmesan cheese, and pine nuts. Here the pesto that's stirred into the pancake batter and gives it its spring-green color and mild, slightly sweet flavor includes basil, oil, and a full head of roasted garlic. (When roasted, garlic becomes meltingly tender, sweet, and almost caramellike.) The Parmesan is part of the batter and the pine nuts are an optional topping.

ABOUT TWENTY-FOUR 2 ½-INCH PANCAKES

1 head garlic

Olive oil for drizzling

2 cups (packed) fresh basil leaves

¼ cup extra-virgin olive oil

1 teaspoon salt

1 cup all-purpose flour

¼ cup freshly grated Parmesan
   cheese

¾ teaspoon baking powder

1 cup vegetable or chicken broth

1 large egg

1 cup toasted pine nuts (optional)

Easy Aïoli (recipe follows)
   for topping

continued

1. Preheat the oven to 325°F. Cut away the top quarter of the garlic head and peel off the loose skin. Place the garlic in the center of a small square of aluminum foil, drizzle with a little olive oil, and pull up the sides of the foil to enclose the garlic. Place the packet on a small baking sheet and roast for 30 to 45 minutes, or until the garlic cloves ooze from their skin when the head is lightly pressed. Open the packet and cool to room temperature. (The garlic can be roasted a few hours ahead and kept at room temperature until needed.)

2. Squeeze the garlic pulp into a blender or a food processor fitted with the metal blade. Add the basil, oil, and salt and process until pureed. Set the pesto aside.

3. In a medium bowl, whisk together the flour, Parmesan, and baking powder. In another bowl, whisk together the broth and egg. Pour the liquid ingredients over the dry ingredients and mix with the whisk, stopping when everything is combined. With a rubber spatula, gently stir in the pesto.

4. If necessary, lightly butter, oil, or spray your griddle or skillet. Preheat over medium heat or, if using an electric griddle, set to 350°F. If you want to hold the pancakes until serving time, preheat your oven to 200°F.

5. Spoon 2 tablespoons of batter onto the griddle for each pancake, allowing space for spreading. If using the pine nuts, sprinkle a few over each pancake before the batter sets. When the undersides of the pancakes are golden and ringed in palest green and the tops are speckled with bubbles that pop and stay open, flip the pancakes over with a wide spatula and cook until the other sides are light brown. Serve immediately, or keep the finished pancakes in the preheated oven while you make the rest of the batch.

Easy Aïoli

Aïoli is a garlic mayonnaise that originated in the south of France. In fact, it has been called the butter of Provence. This recipe is not for an authentic aïoli, which is made with plenty of raw garlic, egg yolks, olive oil, and, often, a boiled potato. Instead, it's a quick and easy version made with store-bought mayonnaise. What makes it distinctive—and easily digestible—is the use of sweet, soft roasted garlic, a whole head of it. If you want to come closer to the texture of genuine aïoli, use homemade mayonnaise.

1 head roasted garlic (see Step 1 on
page 60 for roasting directions)
1 cup mayonnaise

1 teaspoon Dijon mustard
Salt and freshly ground black pepper
to taste

Squeeze the garlic into a blender or a food processor fitted with the metal blade or, if you're using an immersion blender, into a medium bowl. Add the mayonnaise and mustard and blend until the garlic is completely pureed and the mixture is smooth. Add salt and pepper to taste. Spoon into a container with a lid and refrigerate. The aïoli will keep for 3 days.

SERVING: If I'm serving these pancakes with cocktails, I like to fan them out on a large serving platter, place a bowl of Easy Aïoli in the center, and leave the platter on the buffet. With or without the topping, they can replace the bread, rice, or potatoes you'd normally serve with dinner. For a special treat, let the pancakes cool to room temperature and then float them in summer soups like gazpacho, chilled cucumber-yogurt soup, or cold borscht. They're an unexpected and absolutely delicious addition to warm-weather meals.

Spicy Buttermilk Crab Cakes
Topped with Tomato-Crab Salad

These are love-at-first-bite pancakes: big, soft, chewy, chockful of crabmeat, nicely spiced, and fresh-from-the-sea sweet.

1¼ cups all-purpose flour	1 tablespoon Worcestershire sauce
1¼ teaspoons baking powder	¾ teaspoon Tabasco sauce
¼ teaspoon baking soda	6 ounces crabmeat, picked clean of shells
1 teaspoon salt	and cartilage and flaked
Pinch of cayenne	3 scallions, white part only, thinly sliced
1½ cups buttermilk	3 tablespoons minced fresh basil
2 large eggs	
3 tablespoons unsalted butter,	Tomato-Crab Salad (recipe follows)
melted	for topping

1. In a medium bowl, whisk together the flour, baking powder, baking soda, salt, and cayenne. In another bowl, whisk together the buttermilk, eggs, melted butter, Worcestershire, and Tabasco. Pour the liquid ingredients over the dry ingredients and mix with the whisk, stopping when everything is just combined. (Don't worry if the batter is a bit lumpy.) With a rubber spatula, gently but thoroughly fold in the crabmeat, scallions, and basil.
2. If necessary, lightly butter, oil, or spray your griddle or skillet. Preheat over medium heat

or, if using an electric griddle, set to 350°F. If you want to hold the pancakes until serving time, preheat your oven to 200°F.

3. Spoon ⅓ cup of batter onto the griddle for each pancake, allowing space for spreading, and use a spatula or the back of your spoon to lightly press the batter into rounds. (This batter will never spread to perfect rounds.) When the undersides of the pancakes are golden and the tops are speckled with bubbles that pop and stay open, flip the pancakes over with a wide spatula and cook until the other sides are light brown. Serve immediately, or keep the finished pancakes in the preheated oven while you make the rest of the batch.

Tomato-Crab Salad

Even if the pancakes are gobbled up, you can use this salad to stuff a ripe tomato, mound on crackers for snacks, or make the tastiest crabmeat salad sandwich in town.

¾ pound crabmeat, flaked	*Pinch of cayenne*
Juice of ½ lemon	*1 tomato, cored, seeded, and diced*
3 tablespoons mayonnaise	*2 tablespoons minced fresh basil*
2 teaspoons ketchup	*Salt and freshly ground black pepper*
¼ teaspoon Tabasco sauce	*to taste*

Mix the ingredients together gently with a rubber spatula; salt and pepper as needed. Serve immediately or store in a covered container in the refrigerator for up to 1 day.

SERVING: Serve the pancakes topped with the crab salad on plates garnished with thin tomato slices and whole fresh basil leaves.

Sour Cream–Dill Pancakes

These puffy pancakes, with a thick, creamy inner sponge, the crunch of shallots, and the spring freshness of dill, straddle the line between brunch and later-in-the-day meals and snacks, especially when they're topped with smoked fish.

ABOUT TEN 4-INCH PANCAKES

1 cup all-purpose flour

1 teaspoon baking powder

¼ teaspoon baking soda

¾ teaspoon salt

¼ teaspoon freshly ground black
   pepper

¾ cup milk

½ cup sour cream (you can use
   nonfat)

1 large egg

2 tablespoons unsalted butter, melted

1 shallot, minced

¼ cup (packed) snipped fresh dill

Smoked fish, tomato slices, sliced
   red onion, and sour cream
   for topping

1. In a medium bowl, whisk together the flour, baking powder, baking soda, salt, and pepper. In another bowl, whisk together the milk, sour cream, egg, and melted butter. Pour the liquid ingredients over the dry ingredients and mix with the whisk, stopping when everything is just combined. (Don't worry if the batter is a bit lumpy.) With a rubber spatula, gently fold in the minced shallot and dill.

2. If necessary, lightly butter, oil, or spray your griddle or skillet. Preheat over medium heat or, if using an electric griddle, set to 350°F. If you want to hold the pancakes until serving time, preheat your oven to 200°F.

3. Spoon ¼ cup of batter onto the griddle for each pancake, allowing space for spreading, and use a spatula or the back of your spoon to lightly press the batter into rounds. When the undersides of the pancakes are golden and the tops are speckled with bubbles that pop and stay open, flip the pancakes over with a wide spatula and cook until the other sides are light brown. Serve immediately, or keep the finished pancakes in the preheated oven while you make the rest of the batch.

S ERVING : If you want to serve these for brunch, offer a platter with a selection of thinly sliced smoked salmon, chunks of smoked whitefish, and fillets of smoked trout, along with slices of onions and tomatoes and sour cream for topping. When they're destined to be the first course of a meal, allow one pancake for each person and present them on individual plates with the fixings already in place. For canapés, you can make the pancakes silver dollar size. Top each with a dab of sour cream, a bit of smoked fish, a quarter slice of tomato, and a sliver of onion, and serve with chilled white wine, Champagne, or festive kirs.

Matzo Meal Pancakes

These are traditionally served in Jewish households at Passover, the week-long observance during which leavened products are not used. Matzo is unleavened bread—really a cracker—and it is available as meal in most supermarkets year-round.

Sometimes called *latkes*—the Yiddish word for pancakes—these are light and as irresistible as potato chips. One pancake leads to another and another and. . . . They are served before dinner or as dumplings in chicken soup. If you're serving them before dinner, serve them with Homemade Applesauce or let everyone dip the pancakes in sugar, assurance of a sweet Passover.

ABOUT SIXTEEN 2 ½ - INCH PANCAKES

½ cup matzo meal

1 tablespoon sugar

½ teaspoon salt

¼ teaspoon freshly ground black

    pepper

¾ cup hot water

2 large eggs, beaten

Peanut oil for sautéing

Homemade Applesauce (page 46) or

    sugar for topping

1. In a medium bowl, whisk together the matzo meal, sugar, salt, and pepper. In another bowl, whisk together the water and eggs. Pour the liquid ingredients over the dry ingredients and stir just until combined.

2. If you want to keep the pancakes for a short time before serving, preheat your oven to 200°F. Pour enough peanut oil to come ⅛ inch up the sides of a large cast-iron or other heavy skillet and heat over medium heat until the oil is very hot but not bubbling. While the oil is heating, line a baking sheet with a brown paper bag or a triple thickness of paper towels.

3. For each pancake, spoon 1 tablespoon of batter into the hot oil and press down gently with the back of the spoon to create a pancake that's about 2½ inches across. Be careful not to crowd the pan—leave about 2 inches of space between the pancakes. Cook the pancakes until the undersides are pale golden with darker rims, then turn with a wide spatula and a fork and brown the other sides. Lift the pancakes out of the oil, letting the excess oil drip back into the skillet, and place on the brown paper to drain. Pat the tops of the pancakes free of excess oil with paper toweling and serve immediately, or keep them in the warm oven while you make the rest of the batch.

SERVING: While some devotees will eat these at any temperature, I think they're best just out of the skillet, and I love them sprinkled with a light dusting of granulated sugar and served with applesauce. Think of these when you've got a wonderful clear soup, like a homemade chicken soup or beef bouillon. Just float one in the center of each bowl—it makes an interesting alternative to a crouton.

Chickpea Pancakes with Creamy Tahini Topping

When you see the ingredients that go into these unusual pancakes, you'll recognize the basics of hummus, a Middle Eastern creation that is used as both a spread and a flavorful filler for pitas (pocket breads). Indeed, it was the heady aromas and distinctive flavors of hummus—smooth chickpeas, sharp garlic, tangy lemon, and rich tahini—that inspired me to transform this favorite into silver-dollar–size pancakes for passing at cocktail parties or serving as a starter to a special dinner. As exotic as the flavors may seem, the ingredients needed to make these tantalizing cakes and the Creamy Tahini Topping are available in supermarkets.

ABOUT TWENTY 2 ½ -INCH PANCAKES

1 cup canned chickpeas, drained (reserve the liquid)

½ cup tahini (sesame paste)

¼ cup reserved liquid from the chickpeas

3 cloves garlic, peeled

Juice of 2 lemons

2 large eggs

½ teaspoon cumin

1 teaspoon salt

¼ cup all-purpose flour

Creamy Tahini Topping (recipe follows) and tomato slices or cubes for topping

1. Place all the ingredients except the flour in a blender or a food processor fitted with the metal blade. Whirl until the chickpeas and garlic are pureed and the mixture is smooth. Sprinkle over the flour and process just until the flour disappears.

2. If necessary, lightly butter, oil, or spray your griddle or skillet. Preheat over medium heat or, if using an electric griddle, set to 350°F. If you want to hold the pancakes until serving time, preheat your oven to 200°F.

3. Spoon a rounded tablespoon of batter onto the griddle for each pancake, allowing space for spreading. When the undersides of the pancakes are golden and the tops are speckled with bubbles that pop and stay open, flip the pancakes over with a wide spatula and cook until the other sides are light brown. Serve immediately, or keep the finished pancakes in the preheated oven while you make the rest of the batch.

Creamy Tahini Topping

I created this savory mayonnaise-based topping expressly for these chickpea-and-tahini pancakes, but it also makes a fine dressing for cucumber salads or sliced tomatoes.

1 cup mayonnaise	*¼ teaspoon cumin*
1½ tablespoons fresh lemon juice	*½ teaspoon salt*
1 tablespoon tahini	

Place all the ingredients in a small bowl and blend thoroughly with a rubber spatula or electric mixer. Store covered in the refrigerator until ready to serve. The topping will keep for 1 week.

SERVING: The pancakes are at their best warm but can be eaten at room temperature. Top each pancake with Tahini and a slice of tomato. To make these part of a buffet, serve the pancakes fanned out around bowls of topping and diced tomato.

Jalapeño-Corn Cakes with Red Pepper Salsa

I think I could eat these every day for a month and then crave them the next day. They're soft, spicy, and chockablock with corn and corn's irresistible sweetness. They're great whether you dress them up with Red Pepper Salsa, dip them in ready-made barbecue sauce, or munch them straight off the griddle, plain but bursting with flavor. I made these early one day and reheated them in the evening on the outdoor grill—they were terrific. The cooked cornmeal (very much like polenta) took on a crisp crust and the grill's smoke added a subtle, mysterious warmth to the peppers within. Try it the next time you've got the grill fired up. And don't worry if you can't get your hands on fresh corn on the cob—these are still scrumptious made with frozen kernel corn.

ABOUT TWENTY 2 ½ - INCH PANCAKES

1½ cups chicken broth

3 tablespoons corn oil

1 cup yellow cornmeal, preferably stone-ground

2 teaspoons baking powder

2 tablespoons finely minced jalapeño pepper

2 tablespoons finely minced fresh cilantro

3 large eggs, beaten

4 drops Tabasco sauce, or more to taste

1 teaspoon salt, or more to taste

¾ teaspoon freshly ground black pepper

1 cup corn kernels (cut from 1 to 2 ears of corn or thawed frozen)

Red Pepper Salsa (recipe follows) for topping

1. Bring the chicken broth and corn oil to a boil in a medium saucepan. Reduce the heat to medium and gradually add the cornmeal, whisking all the while. Still whisking, cook the cornmeal for 2 minutes. The cornmeal will absorb the liquid and thicken like polenta. Remove the pan from the heat and let cool for about 5 minutes.

2. Whisk the baking powder, jalapeño, cilantro, eggs, Tabasco, salt, and pepper into the cornmeal until well blended. Fold in the corn kernels with a rubber spatula.

3. If necessary, lightly butter, oil, or spray your griddle or skillet. Preheat over medium heat or, if using an electric griddle, set to 350°F. If you want to hold the pancakes until serving time, preheat your oven to 200°F.

4. Spoon ¼ cup of batter onto the griddle for each pancake, allowing space for spreading, and use a spatula or the back of your spoon to lightly press the batter into rounds. When the undersides of the pancakes are golden (you won't see many bubbles on the tops), flip the pancakes over with a wide spatula and cook until the other sides are light brown. Serve immediately, or keep the finished pancakes in the preheated oven while you make the rest of the batch.

continued

Red Pepper Salsa

Jalapeño-Corn Cakes are made for a sparkling, piquant salsa and this one has sparkle to spare. You'll recognize the signature salsa tastes—a combination of jalapeño and cilantro—but I've added a tad of honey to soften the flavors and suggest that you taste as you go along. Salsas are one of those wonderful condiments that take kindly to personal touches—make this one your own by adding more heat (jalapeño, Tabasco, black pepper, or even chili powder), more sweet (honey or sugar), or more accents, such as snipped chives, sliced scallions, or a sprinkling of fresh mint.

2 red bell peppers, cored, seeded, deveined, and cut into small dice

1 small red onion, cut into small dice

1 jalapeño pepper (or less to taste), seeded, deveined, and finely chopped

¼ cup finely chopped fresh cilantro

Juice of 2 limes

½ teaspoon honey

Tabasco sauce to taste

Salt and freshly ground black pepper to taste

Mix all the ingredients together in a medium bowl. The salsa is ready to eat as soon as the ingredients are combined; it can be prepared ahead, covered, and refrigerated for an hour or so, but it won't maintain its freshness and crunch if it's made too far in advance.

Serving: These are great as a buffet offering, a first course (arrange a trio of pancakes on a plate and top each with the colorful salsa), or a side dish with a casual main course like grilled chicken, barbecued ribs, thin-sliced flank steak, or a simple fish preparation.

Creamy, Cheesy, Garlicky Grits Griddle Cakes with Glistening Parsley Drizzle

Delicious and delicate (the grits are barely distinguishable as the breakfast grits most of us know), these pancakes are a delightful addition to both down-home dinners and fancier fare. The Parmesan cheese mixed into the batter results in a golden, crackly crust so the ultrathin pancakes are crispy on the outside and soft, peppery, and garlicky-good inside.

ABOUT SIXTEEN 3-INCH PANCAKES

2 cups water

1 teaspoon salt, or more to taste

¼ cup plus 2 tablespoons grits (not
   instant or quick-cooking)

2 tablespoons unsalted butter,
   at room temperature

½ cup freshly grated Parmesan cheese

3 scallions, white part only, thinly
   sliced

1 to 2 cloves garlic, pressed

1 tablespoon snipped fresh chives
   (optional)

1 tablespoon finely minced parsley
   (optional)

Tabasco sauce to taste

Freshly ground black pepper to taste

Glistening Parsley Drizzle (recipe follows)
   for topping

1. Bring the water and salt to a boil in a medium saucepan. Reduce the heat to medium-low and, whisking all the while, gradually add the grits. Cook over medium-low heat, stirring frequently, for 12 to 15 minutes, until the grits have absorbed the water and are creamy; your whisk should leave a trail on the bottom of the pan when you stir the mixture. Remove the pan from the heat.

2. With a whisk or rubber spatula, stir in the butter, cheese, scallions, and garlic, and chives and parsley if using. This is the kind of mixture that takes a little tasting to get to your liking, so taste the grits and add Tabasco, black pepper, and more salt as you see fit.

3. If necessary, lightly butter, oil, or spray your griddle or skillet. Preheat over medium heat or, if using an electric griddle, set to 350°F. If you want to hold the pancakes until serving time, preheat your oven to 200°F.

4. Spoon about 3 tablespoons of batter onto the griddle for each pancake, allowing space for spreading. When the undersides of the pancakes are well browned and crispy, flip the pancakes over with a wide spatula and cook until the other sides are golden. (The pancakes are quite delicate, so work carefully to get your spatula completely under each pancake and flip the pancakes gently, taking care not to let them crumple.) Serve immediately, or keep the finished pancakes in the preheated oven while you make the rest of the batch.

Glistening Parsley Drizzle

Here's a shimmering thin olive oil and parsley sauce with as much punch as pesto and a little extra zip. It's perfect over Grits Griddle Cakes and well worth keeping in mind the next time you're looking for a light sauce to enliven simple poached, steamed, or grilled fish.

1 cup (packed) flat-leaf Italian parsley leaves

½ clove garlic

1 teaspoon salt, or more to taste

1 cup extra-virgin olive oil

Juice of ½ lemon, or to taste

Place the parsley, garlic, and salt in a blender or a food processor fitted with the metal blade. (This is a good job for an immersion blender, if you have one.) Add half the olive oil and process until the parsley is chopped. With the motor running, add the remaining oil in a steady stream, processing until you have a glistening puree. Transfer to a bowl, taste, and add the lemon juice, adjusting the seasoning as needed. The Drizzle will keep, covered in the refrigerator, for 1 week. Bring to room temperature and shake or stir before serving.

SERVING: Make these the sidekick to any main course that needs a pick-me-up. Serve three or four to a plate and allow diners to dish out the Drizzle for themselves.

Spiced Carrot Pancakes

The spices that give these blini-size pancakes their unusual flavor are reminiscent of curry but softer, more subtle, and harder to pin down. That they're not easily classified only adds to the appeal, as does the fact that the pancakes are thick, beautifully orange-tinged, and elegant in every respect. I love the light crust these get when made in a cast-iron platar, but they are still prime polish-them-off-quickly material made in a skillet or on a griddle.

ABOUT TWENTY 3-INCH PANCAKES

1 pound carrots, peeled and cut into 1-inch-long chunks	1 teaspoon salt
1 cup all-purpose flour	1 cup milk
1½ teaspoons baking powder	1 large egg
¾ teaspoon ground cumin	4 tablespoons (½ stick) unsalted butter, melted
½ teaspoon ground ginger	
¼ teaspoon cayenne	Major Grey or other store-bought spicy
⅛ teaspoon cinnamon	mango chutney for topping

1. Place the carrots in a medium saucepan, cover with water, and bring to a boil. Reduce the heat to medium, partially cover the pan, and cook until the carrots are tender enough to be pierced easily with the tip of a knife. Drain the carrots well and place them in a food processor fitted with the metal blade. Process the carrots, scraping down the sides of the bowl as needed, until you have a smooth puree. Measure out 1 cup of the puree, and reserve any remaining puree for another use. (If you have any leftover puree, it won't be much—

maybe just enough to add a little color and another flavor to mashed potatoes or a root vegetable puree.)

2. In a medium bowl, whisk together the flour, baking powder, cumin, ginger, cayenne, cinnamon, and salt. In another bowl, whisk together the milk, egg, and melted butter to blend thoroughly. Pour the liquid ingredients over the dry ingredients and mix with the whisk, stopping when everything is just combined. With a rubber spatula, gently but thoroughly fold in the carrot puree. You'll have a very thick batter.

3. If necessary, lightly butter, oil, or spray your platar, griddle, or skillet. Preheat over medium heat or, if using an electric griddle, set to 350°F. If you want to hold the pancakes until serving time, preheat your oven to 200°F.

4. Spoon 2 tablespoons of batter onto the platar or griddle for each pancake. If using a platar, gently press down on the batter to help it fill the indentations. If you're using a griddle or skillet, leave room for spreading, and use a spatula or the back of your spoon to lightly press the batter into rounds. When the undersides of the pancakes are golden and the tops are lightly speckled with bubbles that pop and stay open, flip the pancakes over with a spatula and cook until the other sides are light brown. Serve immediately, or keep the finished pancakes in the preheated oven while you make the rest of the batch.

SERVING: These deserve to be served on their own, either as part of a buffet or as a starter. Allow two to three pancakes per person, topping each with some chutney and dressing the plate with a small mound of frilly herb salad or mesclun moistened with a mustard vinaigrette.

Blini

The real thing. Well, almost. These bready, lightly nut-flavored, chocolate milk–colored pancakes are not as buckwheaty as traditional Russian blini—all the better for blending with the briny flavors of caviar and smoked fish. You can make these on a griddle, but I like to use a platar because it turns out blinis that are just the right size for a dollop of crème fraîche and an oversize spoonful of caviar. Because they are yeast-raised, blini take longer to make than ordinary pancakes, but they're no more difficult to put together than any other flapjack and so much more elegant than any other edible underpinning for caviar, perfect for celebrations.

ABOUT THIRTY-FIVE 3-INCH PANCAKES

1½ cups milk	*½ teaspoon salt*
4 tablespoons (½ stick) unsalted	*3 large eggs, beaten*
butter, cut into 4 pieces	
2 teaspoons active dry yeast	
¾ cup all-purpose flour	*Caviar or smoked fish, such as salmon or*
½ cup buckwheat flour	*trout, and Crème Fraîche (page 51) or*
2 tablespoons sugar	*sour cream for topping*

1. Place the milk and butter in a saucepan and warm over medium heat just until the butter is melted and the milk is about 110°F (or the maximum temperature for liquid indicated on your packet of yeast), but no hotter. While the mixture is heating, whisk together the yeast, all-purpose and buckwheat flours, sugar, and salt in a medium bowl.

2. Pour the warm milk-butter mixture over the dry ingredients and stir with the whisk to blend. Cover the bowl with plastic wrap and place in a warm draft-free spot to rise until doubled in bulk, 1 to 1½ hours.

3. When the mixture is bubbly and doubled in bulk, you can either make the pancakes or place the covered bowl in the refrigerator until you're ready to cook them. Chilled, the batter will keep for a day; if you've chilled the batter, allow it to sit at room temperature for 20 minutes before proceeding.

4. Stir the batter down and stir in the beaten eggs.

5. If necessary, lightly butter, oil, or spray your platar, griddle, or skillet. Preheat over medium heat or, if using an electric griddle, set to 350°F. If you want to hold the blini until serving time, preheat your oven to 200°F.

6. Spoon 2 tablespoons of the batter onto the platar or griddle for each blini. If you're using a griddle or skillet, leave room for spreading. When the undersides of the pancakes are golden and the tops are speckled with bubbles that pop and stay open, flip the blini over with a spatula and cook until the other sides are light brown. Serve immediately, or keep the finished pancakes in the preheated oven while you make the rest of the batch.

S E R V I N G :   Often blini are served with pressed caviar, an intensely flavored thick caviar "marmalade" made from crushed caviar berries, but these will be superb with caviar of any kind, from beluga to large, pop-in-your-mouth salmon caviar—or with sleek slices of smoked salmon or trout or rosettes of homey chopped herring salad. Serve with crème fraîche or sour cream. Or, if you want to enjoy the full, rich flavors of the blini solo, just pass some melted butter.

John Bennett's
Beet and Carrot Pancakes

Oklahoma caterer John Bennett makes these silver-dollar–size pancakes often for parties large and small. When I say large, I mean it. I remember talking on the phone to John while he flipped Beet and Carrot Pancakes for five hundred. What makes these pancakes perfect for a caterer makes them just right for home cooks too: They can be made in advance and reheated, and their flavor is blendable, going as well with ritzy caviar and smoked fish as with down-to-earth sour cream and chopped vegetables.

ABOUT TWENTY-FOUR 3-INCH PANCAKES

1 cup all-purpose flour

1 tablespoon sugar

1½ teaspoons baking powder

1 teaspoon baking soda

½ teaspoon salt

¼ teaspoon freshly ground black
   pepper

¼ teaspoon cayenne, or to taste

1 tablespoon grated orange zest

1 tablespoon finely snipped fresh
   chives

1 tablespoon minced fresh dill

¾ cup milk

½ cup heavy cream

1 large egg

3 tablespoons unsalted butter, melted

2 tablespoons fresh orange juice

½ cup grated carrots (about 1 carrot)

½ cup grated beets (about 1 beet)

Crème Fraîche (page 51) or sour cream
   and caviar or smoked salmon
   for topping

1. In a medium bowl, whisk together the flour, sugar, baking powder, baking soda, salt, black pepper, and cayenne. Whisk in the zest, chives, and dill. In another bowl, whisk together the milk, cream, egg, melted butter, and orange juice to blend thoroughly. Pour the liquid ingredients over the dry ingredients and mix with the whisk, stopping when everything is just combined. With a rubber spatula, gently fold in the grated carrots and beets.

2. If necessary, lightly butter, oil, or spray your platar, griddle, or skillet. Preheat over medium heat or, if using an electric griddle, set to 350°F. If you want to hold the pancakes until serving time, preheat your oven to 200°F.

3. Spoon 2 tablespoons of batter onto the platar or griddle for each pancake. If you're using a griddle or skillet, leave room for spreading. When the undersides of the pancakes are golden and the tops are speckled with bubbles that pop and stay open, flip the pancakes over with a spatula and cook until the other sides are light brown. Serve immediately, or keep the finished pancakes in the preheated oven while you make the rest of the batch.

N O T E :   John Bennett always makes these ahead of time. As they come off the platar, he places them on lightly buttered or sprayed baking sheets. When they're cool, he covers them with plastic wrap and stores them in the refrigerator. At serving time, he brushes the pancakes generously with melted butter and runs them under the broiler to heat and crisp.

S E R V I N G :   Colorful Beet and Carrot Pancakes are great with a dollop of crème fraîche or sour cream and a piece of thinly sliced salmon or a spoonful of fresh caviar. If you're feeling flush, think about topping each pancake with salmon *and* caviar.

3

CHAPTER

Poshcakes

Dessert Pancakes

. . . .

Peanut Butter–Chocolate Chip Pancakes with Cinnamon Ice Cream

Pancakes to rival the fun and flavor of all-American peanut butter cookies, these are big, soft, sweet, nutty, and full of gooey melted chocolate chips. And they're not for kids only. In fact, kids will count themselves lucky if grown-ups leave them any.

ABOUT FOURTEEN 5-INCH PANCAKES

1 cup all-purpose flour	4 tablespoons (½ stick) unsalted butter, melted
¼ cup sugar	
2 teaspoons baking powder	1½ cups semisweet chocolate chips
1 teaspoon cinnamon	
½ cup peanut butter (creamy or chunky)	
	Cinnamon Ice Cream (recipe follows) and
2 large eggs	Dark Chocolate Sauce (page 106)
1¼ cups milk	(optional) for topping

1. In a medium bowl, whisk together the flour, sugar, baking powder, and cinnamon. In another bowl, beat the peanut butter and eggs with an electric mixer until softened and well combined. (You can do this by hand with a sturdy rubber spatula; all you need is elbow grease—peanut butter is stiff and sticky and takes a little work to soften.) Gradually add the milk and melted butter, beating until well blended. Use a rubber spatula to stir in the dry ingredients, then gently fold in the chocolate chips.

2. If necessary, lightly butter, oil, or spray your griddle or skillet. Preheat over medium heat or, if using an electric griddle, set to 350°F. (The griddle must not be hotter than 350°F, or you'll risk burning the chocolate chips.) If you want to hold the pancakes until serving time, preheat your oven to 200°F.

3. Spoon ⅓ cup of batter onto the griddle for each pancake, allowing space for spreading, and use a spatula or the back of your spoon to lightly press the batter into rounds. When the undersides of the pancakes are golden and the tops are speckled with bubbles that pop and stay open, flip the pancakes over with a wide spatula and cook until the other sides are light brown. Serve immediately, or keep the finished pancakes in the preheated oven while you make the rest of the batch. Stir the batter between batches to distribute the chocolate chips evenly—they have a tendency to sink to the bottom of the bowl.

continued

Cinnamon Ice Cream

This recipe makes a quart of old-fashioned ice cream with the spicy edge of cinnamon. You'll have enough to serve with these pancakes (add Dark Chocolate Sauce for a pancake sundae) and some left over to pair with a batch of Coffee-Time Pancakes (page 99).

3 cups milk	1 cup sugar
1 cup heavy cream	1 tablespoon cinnamon
6 large egg yolks	1 teaspoon pure vanilla extract

1. Bring the milk and cream to a boil in a medium heavy-bottomed saucepan. While the mixture is heating, use a whisk or an electric mixer to beat the egg yolks, sugar, and cinnamon together in a medium bowl until very thick.

2. Beating constantly, gradually add the hot milk and cream to the yolk mixture. Return the mixture to the saucepan and cook over medium heat, stirring constantly with a wooden spoon, until the custard thickens, 2 to 5 minutes. The custard should coat the wooden spoon and when you run your finger down the bowl of the spoon, it should leave a track. Strain into a clean bowl. Stir in the vanilla extract and cool to room temperature.

3. Freeze the custard in an ice cream maker following the manufacturer's instructions. Pack into a freezer container and freeze to firm and ripen. The ice cream should be ready to scoop in about 2 hours, but it will keep in the freezer for 2 weeks.

SERVING: Stack a couple of pancakes in the center of a large plate, add a hefty scoop of ice cream, and pour over some Dark Chocolate Sauce if you'd like.

Rice Pudding Pancakes
with Rum Custard Sauce

Creamy rum-rich rice pudding with raisins forms the batter for these delicate pancakes with a dark, crispy crust. They make an elegant finish to a dinner party or an indulgent addition to a weekend brunch. Give them a gloss of Rum Custard Sauce and you will have created a dessert for gastronomic hedonists.

ABOUT TWENTY-FOUR 3-INCH PANCAKES

½ cup long-grain white rice

3 cups milk

¼ cup sugar

¼ cup all-purpose flour

½ teaspoon baking powder

¼ teaspoon baking soda

½ cup sour cream

2 large eggs, beaten

2 tablespoons unsalted butter, melted

2 tablespoons dark rum

1 teaspoon pure vanilla extract

¼ teaspoon pure almond extract

1 cup plump raisins

Rum Custard Sauce (recipe follows)
*   for topping*

1. Place the rice in a medium saucepan and stir in the milk and sugar. Bring to a boil over medium heat, stirring often (keep a watchful eye on the pot because the mixture has a tendency to bubble over). Lower the heat to a simmer and cook, stirring occasionally, until most of the milk is absorbed and just a thin film remains, 35 to 40 minutes. Remove from the heat and cool for about 20 minutes, stirring now and then.

continued

87

2. In a small bowl, whisk together the flour, baking powder, and baking soda. Then whisk the sour cream, beaten eggs, melted butter, rum, and extracts into the rice. Add the flour mixture to the rice and stir with a rubber spatula just until everything is combined. Gently fold in the raisins.

3. If necessary, lightly butter, oil, or spray your griddle or skillet. Preheat over medium heat or, if using an electric griddle, set to 350°F. If you want to hold the pancakes until serving time, preheat your oven to 200°F.

4. Spoon 3 tablespoons of batter onto the griddle for each pancake, allowing space for spreading, and use a spatula or the back of your spoon to nudge the batter into rounds. When the undersides of the pancakes are golden and the tops are speckled with bubbles that pop and stay open, flip the pancakes over with a wide spatula and cook until the other sides are light brown. (These pancakes are very soft and not easy to flip: Get your spatula under as much of each pancake as you can and flip with determination, taking care not to let the pancake fold over on itself.) Serve immediately, or keep the finished pancakes in the preheated oven while you make the rest of the batch.

Rum Custard Sauce

Rum Custard Sauce is smooth, silky, sophisticated, and easy to make. It is a simple crème anglaise, or pouring custard, that can be made a couple of days ahead and presented when needed to give pancakes more polish.

1 cup milk	*1 tablespoon dark rum*
3 large egg yolks	*1 teaspoon pure vanilla extract*
¼ cup sugar	*¼ teaspoon pure almond extract*

1. In a small heavy-bottomed saucepan, bring the milk to a boil. While the milk is heating, whisk the yolks and sugar together in a medium bowl until thick and pale.

2. Whisking constantly, add about ¼ cup of the boiling milk to the yolks. Whisk in the rest of the milk, then return the mixture to the saucepan. Cook the mixture over medium heat, whisking constantly, until slightly thickened. One bubble may pop at the surface, but the mixture must not boil.

3. When the custard is thickened, strain it into a clean bowl. Stir in the rum and vanilla and almond extracts. Cool the sauce to room temperature, whisking occasionally, then cover and chill. The sauce can be kept in the refrigerator for up to 2 days.

SERVING: Allow four small pancakes per serving, pouring over Rum Custard Sauce in a thin stream and garnishing the plates with fresh berries and candied orange peel or, if you have it on hand, drizzling a little Raspberry Coulis (page 109) in an attractive pattern over the plate. Pass any leftover Rum Custard Sauce in a small pitcher.

continued

Pumpkin Pie Pancakes with Spiced Pumpkin Ice Cream

These are, indeed, pancakes, not pumpkin pie, but they contain many of the ingredients that evoke the delights of that dessert and the holiday season. Their aroma, heady from pumpkin, cinnamon, ginger, and rum, is alluring, their texture soft, and their taste, warms-you-on-a-chilly-night spicy. Pumpkin lovers will recognize all these qualities from their beloved pie, while those less enamored of the holiday squash—or less familiar with its virtues—are apt to adore these pancakes without ever identifying their main ingredient. These are easy to love topped with just a shimmer of maple syrup, but for special occasions, you will want to make the Spiced Pumpkin Ice Cream.

ABOUT SIXTEEN 4 ½ -INCH PANCAKES

1 cup all-purpose flour	1⅓ cups buttermilk
¼ cup granulated sugar	2 large eggs
3 tablespoons (packed) brown sugar	4 tablespoons (½ stick) unsalted butter,
1½ teaspoons baking powder	melted
½ teaspoon baking soda	2 tablespoons dark rum
1 teaspoon cinnamon	1 teaspoon pure vanilla extract
1 teaspoon ground ginger	¾ cup canned solid-pack pumpkin
⅛ teaspoon freshly grated nutmeg	
Pinch of cloves	Spiced Pumpkin Ice Cream (recipe follows)
Pinch of salt	or maple syrup for topping

1. In a medium bowl, whisk together the flour, granulated sugar, brown sugar, baking powder, baking soda, spices, and salt. In another bowl, whisk together the buttermilk, eggs, melted butter, rum, and vanilla to blend thoroughly. Pour the liquid ingredients over the dry ingredients and mix with the whisk, stopping when everything is just combined. (Don't worry if the batter is a bit lumpy.) With a rubber spatula, gently but thoroughly fold in the pumpkin puree.

2. If necessary, lightly butter, oil, or spray your griddle or skillet. Preheat over medium heat or, if using an electric griddle, set to 350°F. If you want to hold the pancakes until serving time, preheat your oven to 200°F.

3. Spoon ¼ cup of batter onto the griddle for each pancake, allowing space for spreading. When the undersides of the pancakes are golden and the tops are lightly speckled with bubbles that pop and stay open, flip the pancakes over with a wide spatula and cook until the other sides are light brown. (These are soft and puffy, so turn carefully.) Serve immediately, or keep the finished pancakes in the preheated oven while you make the rest of the batch.

Spiced Pumpkin Ice Cream

A frozen echo of Pumpkin Pie Pancakes' spices and aromas.

2 cups heavy cream	*¾ teaspoon cinnamon*
2 cups milk	*¼ teaspoon freshly grated nutmeg*
1 cup sugar	*1¼ cups canned solid-pack pumpkin*
8 large egg yolks	*1 teaspoon pure vanilla extract*
1½ teaspoons ground ginger	*2 tablespoons dark rum*

continued

1. Combine the cream, milk, and ½ cup of the sugar in a medium heavy-bottomed saucepan and bring to a boil over medium heat, stirring occasionally. Meanwhile, in a large bowl, whisk the yolks, the remaining ½ cup sugar, and the spices until very thick.

2. Gradually whisk the hot cream mixture into the yolk mixture. Return the mixture to the saucepan and cook over medium-low heat, stirring constantly with a wooden spoon, until the custard thickens, about 5 minutes; do not let the custard boil. When you draw your finger across the back of the spoon, it should leave a track. Strain the custard into a large clean bowl. Add the pumpkin and vanilla extract and whisk to blend. Let cool to room temperature.

3. Freeze the custard in an ice cream maker following the manufacturer's instructions. When the ice cream is almost ready, add the dark rum and process until finished.

4. Pack into a freezer container and freeze to firm and ripen. The ice cream should be ready to scoop in about 2 hours, but it will keep in the freezer for 2 weeks.

SERVING: Don't make these pancakes and their sumptuously spiced ice cream a holiday-only recipe—they're winners whether it's fall or winter, holiday or workday. Serve the pancakes piping hot with a scoop of ice cream melting into them or stack them in an overlapping circle on each plate and drizzle them with pure maple syrup. They'd be just right after a traditional turkey dinner with all the fixings and just as appropriate—and as lip-smacking good—capping a simple supper of poached fish.

Light Lemon Pancakes
with Thick Lemon Curd

Light, lemony, and luscious, these pancakes get their pucker power from lots of grated lemon zest and a shot of tart lemon extract, the most concentrated lemon flavoring you can find. Save these for a refreshing finish to a full-flavored meal.

ABOUT TEN 4-INCH PANCAKES

1 cup all-purpose flour

⅓ cup sugar

1¼ teaspoons baking powder

Pinch of salt

Grated zest of 1 lemon

1 cup milk

1 large egg

3 tablespoons unsalted butter,
melted

1 teaspoon pure vanilla extract

½ teaspoon pure lemon extract

Thick Lemon Curd (recipe follows)
for topping

Fresh berries and Raspberry Coulis
(page 109) for garnish

1. In a medium bowl, whisk together the flour, sugar, baking powder, and salt. Whisk in the lemon zest. In another bowl, whisk together the milk, egg, melted butter, and vanilla and lemon extracts to blend thoroughly. Pour the liquid ingredients over the dry ingredients and mix with the whisk, stopping when everything is just combined. (Don't worry if the batter is a bit lumpy.)

continued

2. If necessary, lightly butter, oil, or spray your griddle or skillet. Preheat over medium heat or, if using an electric griddle, set to 350°F. If you want to hold the pancakes until serving time, preheat your oven to 200°F.

3. Spoon ¼ cup of batter onto the griddle for each pancake, allowing space for spreading. When the undersides of the pancakes are golden and the tops are speckled with bubbles that pop and stay open, flip the pancakes over with a wide spatula and cook until the other sides are light brown. Serve immediately, or keep the finished pancakes in the preheated oven while you make the rest of the batch.

Thick Lemon Curd

If you're short on time, you can buy good-quality imported lemon curd in supermarkets and specialty stores, but homemade lemon curd, sunshine-yellow, buttery, and tart, is very simple and satisfying to make. It is, in fact, the kind of confection that lends itself to being packed into jars, wrapped with gingham and bows, and offered as a gift from your kitchen.

1¼ cups sugar	*1 large egg*
6 tablespoons unsalted butter,	*6 large egg yolks*
cut into tablespoon-size pieces	*Juice of 4 lemons*

Put all the ingredients in a medium heavy-bottomed saucepan and stir with a wooden spoon to moisten the sugar. Place over medium-low heat and cook, stirring constantly, until the butter has melted and the mixture thickens like custard, about 4 to 6 minutes; don't take your eyes off the pan, because the mixture can curdle quickly. When the curd has thickened slightly (it will thicken more as it cools) and you can run your finger along the length of the spoon's bowl and leave a track, pour it into a bowl or jar. Press a piece of plastic wrap against the surface and cool to room temperature. Refrigerate until needed. Packed into a tightly covered jar, the curd will keep for up to 3 months.

SERVING: Unless dinner has been substantial, I'd figure on two pancakes per person. You can either present them as a stack, sandwiched with lemon curd and topped with a small circle of curd, an attractive drizzle of Raspberry Coulis, and some berries for panache, or arrange the pancakes with one overlapping the other just a bit, place the curd in the center, pour the coulis around the edge of the plate, and scatter some fresh berries over all. Either way, you'll have a knock-out dessert.

Tropical Cakes with Golden Mango Sauce

It's the blending of warm flavors like coconut milk, rum, and vanilla with the bright, fresh taste of mango that makes these the culinary counterpart of sunshine and sea breezes. Light, lacy, brown-topped Tropical Cakes are, indeed, very much like cakes: They have a butter-rich aroma, a delicate crumb, and the fullness of a fine tea cake. They're a late-afternoon luxury with a pool of Golden Mango Sauce; add a scattering of diced fresh mango and a drizzle of Raspberry Coulis if you have some on hand.

ABOUT FOURTEEN 4 ½ - INCH CAKES

1 ripe mango	*1½ teaspoons pure vanilla extract*
1 cup all-purpose flour	*½ cup shredded coconut*
½ cup sugar	
1½ teaspoons baking powder	
1½ cups unsweetened coconut milk	*Golden Mango Sauce (recipe follows)*
2 large eggs	*for topping*
4 tablespoons (½ stick) unsalted	*Diced fresh mango (see Step 4) and*
butter, melted	*Raspberry Coulis (page 109) for garnish*
2 tablespoons dark rum	*(optional)*

1. Peel the mango and slice it in half lengthwise to remove the fruit from the pit. Cut each half lengthwise into thin slices and then cut the slices crosswise in half; set aside.

2. In a medium bowl, whisk together the flour, sugar, and baking powder. In another bowl, whisk together the coconut milk, eggs, melted butter, rum, and vanilla extract. Pour the liquid ingredients over the dry ingredients and mix with the whisk, stopping when everything is just combined. (Don't worry if the batter is a bit lumpy.) With a rubber spatula, gently but thoroughly fold in the shredded coconut.

3. If necessary, lightly butter, oil, or spray your griddle or skillet. Preheat over medium heat or, if using an electric griddle, set to 350°F. If you want to hold the pancakes until serving time, preheat your oven to 200°F.

4. Spoon ¼ cup of batter onto the griddle for each pancake, allowing space for spreading. Arrange a few slices of mango on each pancake. (If you have any leftover mango slices, you can dice them and use them for garnish.) When the undersides of the pancakes are golden and the tops are speckled with bubbles that pop and stay open, flip the pancakes over with a wide spatula and cook until the other sides are light brown. Serve immediately, or keep the finished pancakes in the preheated oven while you make the rest of the batch.

continued

Golden Mango Sauce

A blender makes fast work of this smooth, shiny mango sauce with its lively citrus accents. The recipe makes one cup of sauce; double it if you wish—it would perk up Basic Pancakes (page 2) and be unorthodox but swell as a sauce for crêpes, either sweet (page 128) or buckwheat (page 118).

1 ripe mango
Juice of 1 lime

2 tablespoons honey

Place all the ingredients in a blender or a food processor fitted with the metal blade and whirl until the puree is perfectly smooth. Cover and refrigerate until ready to serve. The sauce will keep for about 4 days.

SERVING: This would make a fine dessert after an outdoor dinner or the right sweet for an afternoon tea. Place a double or triple stack of pancakes on each plate, spreading each pancake with some of the Golden Mango Sauce. Top the stack with diced fresh mango, drizzle over Raspberry Coulis, and serve with either black coffee or fruit-flavored tea.

Coffee-Time Pancakes

Made with coffee—and ideal for a coffee break—these pancakes are soft and thin with a come-hither aroma, an appealing caramel sweetness, and a color reminiscent of café au lait. I make them large in order to have enough room on top for a generous scoop of ice cream, but you could make twice as many at half the size and serve several to a plate.

ABOUT EIGHT 5 ½ -INCH PANCAKES

1 cup all-purpose flour

½ cup sugar

1 teaspoon baking powder

1 tablespoon instant espresso
powder (not freeze-dried)

¼ teaspoon cinnamon

Pinch of salt

½ cup strong brewed coffee, cooled
to room temperature

½ cup milk

1 large egg

3 tablespoons unsalted butter, melted

Dark Chocolate Sauce (page 106) and
premium-quality coffee ice cream
for topping

Shaved chocolate for garnish (optional)

1. In a medium bowl, whisk together the flour, sugar, baking powder, espresso powder, cinnamon, and salt. In another bowl, whisk together the coffee, milk, egg, and melted butter to blend thoroughly. Pour the liquid ingredients over the dry ingredients and mix with the whisk, stopping when everything is just combined. (Don't worry if the batter is a bit lumpy.)

continued

2. If necessary, lightly butter, oil, or spray your griddle or skillet. Preheat over medium heat or, if using an electric griddle, set to 350°F. If you want to hold the pancakes until serving time, preheat your oven to 200°F.

3. Spoon ¼ cup of batter onto the griddle for each pancake, allowing plenty of space for spreading. When the undersides of the pancakes are golden and the tops are speckled with bubbles that pop and stay open, flip the pancakes over with a wide spatula and cook until the other sides are light brown. (Take extra care with the flipping, since these pancakes are very thin and soft.) Serve immediately, or keep the finished pancakes in the preheated oven while you make the rest of the batch.

SERVING: Working under the theory that too much of a good thing is almost enough, I like to nap each plate with Dark Chocolate Sauce, put the pancakes on top of the sauce, center a scoop of coffee ice cream on the pancakes, and then sprinkle the plate with shavings of imported bittersweet chocolate. The combination is celestial. Of course, if you're looking for a change of pace, you can play around with these, topping them with hot fudge sauce and replacing the coffee ice cream with Cinnamon Ice Cream (page 86), adding chocolate chips to the batter and scooping chocolate ice cream onto the hot cakes, or serving them with a butterscotch sauce that will pick up the caramel flavors.

Gingerbread Pancakes
with Port-Poached Pears

All the pleasures and goodness of the best gingerbread are packed into these pancakes. They've got plenty of spice and they're soft and sweet with a texture that recalls an ultra-light cake or an airy soufflé. Served piping hot with elegant ruby-red Port-Poached Pears, they'll bring back the joys of Christmases past.

ABOUT TWELVE 4 ½-INCH PANCAKES

1 cup all-purpose flour

⅓ cup (packed) brown sugar

1½ teaspoons baking powder

¼ teaspoon baking soda

2 teaspoons ground ginger

½ teaspoon cinnamon

½ teaspoon dry mustard

Pinch of ground cloves

Pinch of freshly grated nutmeg

¼ teaspoon salt

¾ cup sour cream (you can use nonfat)

½ cup milk

4 tablespoons (½ stick) unsalted butter, melted

2 tablespoons molasses

1 large egg

Port-Poached Pears (recipe follows) for topping

1. In a medium bowl, whisk together the flour, brown sugar, baking powder, baking soda, spices and salt, making sure the brown sugar does not clump. In another bowl, whisk together the sour cream, milk, melted butter, molasses, and egg to blend thoroughly. Pour the liquid ingredients over the dry ingredients and mix with the whisk, stopping when everything is just combined. (Don't worry if the batter is a bit lumpy.)

2. If necessary, lightly butter, oil, or spray your griddle or skillet. Preheat over medium heat or, if using an electric griddle, set to 350°F. If you want to hold the pancakes until serving time, preheat your oven to 200°F.

3. Spoon ¼ cup of batter onto the griddle for each pancake, allowing space for spreading, and use a spatula or the back of your spoon to lightly press the batter into rounds. When the undersides of the pancakes are very brown and the tops are lightly speckled with bubbles that pop and stay open, flip the pancakes over with a wide spatula and cook until the other sides are light brown. Serve immediately, or keep the finished pancakes in the preheated oven while you make the rest of the batch.

Port-Poached Pears

This recipe will give you elegant, ruby-red pears, a sensuously spiced syrup, and a house filled with an extraordinary welcoming aroma.

¼ cup fresh lemon juice
8 large firm but ripe pears,
  preferably with stems
4 cups ruby port
2 cups sugar

15 slices peeled fresh ginger, each the size
  of a quarter
2 cinnamon sticks
1 vanilla bean, split lengthwise

1. Fill a large bowl with cold water and add the lemon juice. Peel the pears, leaving the stems intact. Using a melon baller, remove the cores by working your way up through the bottom ends. As each pear is peeled, place it in the bowl of acidulated water.

2. Combine the port, sugar, ginger, cinnamon sticks, and vanilla bean in a large heavy pot (a Dutch oven is perfect) and bring to a boil over high heat, stirring until the sugar is dissolved. Reduce the heat to medium-low and simmer the syrup for 10 minutes.

3. Drain the pears and add them to the syrup. Simmer until tender, turning frequently, about 20 minutes. Use a slotted spoon to transfer the pears to a large container, standing them upright.

4. Boil the syrup until reduced to 1¾ cups, 15 to 20 minutes. Pour it over the pears, cover, cool to room temperature and then chill. The pears will keep in the refrigerator for about 2 days.

SERVING: These are wonderful whether you serve them as dessert after a festive meal, in the afternoon as a pick-me-up, or late at night when you and your friends come in from the movies and want something special. They are most glamorous with Port-Poached Pears, but are also delicious with just a drizzle of warmed maple syrup and a scoop of store-bought vanilla ice cream. You'll find that Gingerbread Pancakes go well with espresso, mulled cider, or hot honeyed tea and that, while they're at their best hot off the griddle, they've got so much flavor you can even enjoy them at room temperature.

Chocolate Pancakes
with Dark Chocolate Sauce

Chocolate through and through. Soft, rich, and full-flavored enough to satisfy any choco-holic's cravings, these deliver a devil's food cake's deep fudginess and a pancake's pleasing comfort. Make these small enough and they'll be like chocolate snaps. But whatever size you make them, use a great cocoa powder, one that has been Dutch-processed to make it milder and darker.

ABOUT TWENTY 3-INCH PANCAKES

1 cup all-purpose flour

½ cup sugar

⅓ cup unsweetened Dutch-
  processed cocoa (such as
  Droste or Hershey's European
  Style), strained if lumpy

1½ teaspoons baking powder

⅛ teaspoon salt

1 cup milk

1 large egg

4 tablespoons (½ stick) unsalted butter,
  melted

1 teaspoon pure vanilla extract

Dark Chocolate Sauce (recipe follows) and
  premium-quality vanilla or coffee
  ice cream for topping

1. In a medium bowl, whisk together the flour, sugar, cocoa powder, baking powder, and salt. In another bowl, whisk together the milk, egg, melted butter, and vanilla to blend thoroughly. Pour the liquid ingredients over the dry ingredients and mix with the whisk, stopping when everything is just combined. (Don't worry if the batter is a bit lumpy.)

104

2. Lightly butter, oil, or spray your griddle or skillet, even if it has a nonstick surface. (Butter the griddle after each batch only if needed.) Preheat over medium heat or, if using an electric griddle, set to 350°F. If you want to hold the pancakes until serving time, preheat your oven to 200°F.

3. Spoon 3 tablespoons of batter onto the griddle for each pancake, allowing space for spreading, and use a spatula or the back of your spoon to lightly press the batter into rounds. When the undersides of the pancakes are brown and the tops are speckled with bubbles that pop and stay open, flip the pancakes over with a wide spatula and cook until the other sides are light brown. (Flip these pancakes gently; they're soft and thin and need a little extra TLC.) Serve immediately, or keep the finished pancakes in the preheated oven while you make the rest of the batch.

continued

Dark Chocolate Sauce

Here's a shiny, easily pourable, not-too-sweet sauce that's unabashedly chocolaty but polite enough not to overpower its fudgy companion.

3 ounces best-quality bittersweet chocolate, very finely chopped

½ cup heavy cream

½ cup milk

2 teaspoons sugar

½ teaspoon instant espresso powder (not freeze-dried)

Pinch of salt

1 tablespoon unsalted butter, at room temperature

1. Place the chocolate in a heatproof bowl or large measuring cup; set aside.

2. In a medium saucepan, mix the cream, milk, sugar, espresso powder, and salt together and bring to a boil over medium heat, stirring to dissolve the sugar. Remove from the heat and gradually whisk into the chocolate until absolutely smooth. Whisk in the butter. Serve or cover and chill until needed. The sauce will keep for up to 2 weeks; if desired, warm the sauce over low heat or in a microwave oven before using.

SERVING: Count on four pancakes per person even if someone says, "No, I couldn't possibly." Trust me, these go in a flash. Serve the pancakes warm with Dark Chocolate Sauce and, if your conscience allows you, add a big round ball of premium vanilla or coffee ice cream.

Hazelnut Pancakes
with Raspberry Coulis

Hazelnuts, sometimes called filberts, are regal nuts. Their flavor is slightly bitter and supremely adult, and their texture, firm but buttery, is splendid. For this recipe, the nuts are pulverized and used as flour. The butter normally melted for making pancakes is cooked until it's a honey brown. The combination is cozy, indulgent, and luxurious. If an evening in front of a fireplace had a taste, this would be it.

ABOUT TWENTY 4-INCH PANCAKES

4 tablespoons (½ stick) unsalted	*1 cup milk*
butter	*2 large eggs*
½ cup hazelnuts, skinned	*½ teaspoon pure vanilla extract*
⅓ cup sugar	*¼ teaspoon pure almond extract*
1 cup all-purpose flour	
1¼ teaspoons baking powder	
⅛ teaspoon freshly grated nutmeg	*Raspberry Coulis (recipe follows)*
Dash of salt	*for topping*

1. Melt the butter in a small saucepan over low heat. Continue cooking, keeping a watchful eye on the pan, until the butter turns a deep, dark, nutty brown. The butter should become very brown and there will be some solid bits in the pan—that's OK—but you must not let it burn. Set the pan aside.

continued

2. Put the hazelnuts and sugar in a food processor fitted with the metal blade and process to pulverize the nuts. Don't worry if small bits of nuts remain—it's better to have a few crunchy pieces of nut than to turn the mass into hazelnut butter, which is what you will get if you process the mixture too long. Transfer the nuts and sugar to a medium bowl, add the flour, baking powder, nutmeg, and salt, and whisk to combine.

3. In another bowl, whisk together the milk, eggs, extracts, and brown butter, scraping the dark bits from the bottom of the pan into the bowl. Pour the liquid ingredients over the dry ingredients and mix with the whisk, stopping when everything is just combined. (Don't worry if the batter is a bit lumpy.)

4. If necessary, lightly butter, oil, or spray your griddle or skillet. Preheat over medium heat or, if using an electric griddle, set to 350°F. If you want to hold the pancakes until serving time, preheat your oven to 200°F.

5. Spoon 2 tablespoons of batter onto the griddle for each pancake, allowing ample space for spreading. When the undersides of the pancakes are very brown and the tops are lightly speckled with bubbles that pop and stay open, flip the pancakes over with a wide spatula and cook until the other sides are light brown. Serve immediately, or keep the finished pancakes in the preheated oven while you make the rest of the batch.

Raspberry Coulis

A coulis is a pureed sauce, and this coulis is one of the most versatile you can have in your dessert repertoire. You'll pour this over the Hazelnut Pancakes, drizzle some over Tropical Cakes with Golden Mango Sauce (page 98), and use the leftovers to enliven ice creams, cakes, and puddings. This coulis knows no season—if you can't get fresh raspberries, you can use frozen. And, depending on what you're serving the coulis with, you can add a complementary liqueur for extra interest. Playing around with this sauce is easy.

½ pint (about 1¼ cups) fresh or unthawed frozen unsweetened raspberries

2 tablespoons sugar, or more to taste

1 teaspoon fresh lemon juice, or more to taste

2 teaspoons Grand Marnier or other orange liqueur (optional)

Puree the berries with the sugar and lemon juice in a blender or a food processor fitted with the metal blade. Taste and add more sugar and/or lemon juice if needed. Add the liqueur. Pour into a covered container and chill until ready to serve. The coulis can be made up to 1 day in advance.

SERVING: Serve these hot off the griddle and simply, with just a drizzle of Raspberry Coulis, and make sure the espresso is fresh and strong. If you want to dress these up, spread each one with a little melted bittersweet chocolate and a spoonful of lightly sweetened Crème Fraîche (page 51). Then make three-pancake-high towers, topping each one with more chocolate, a dollop of crème fraîche, some berries, a rivulet of Raspberry Coulis, and a shower of finely chopped toasted hazelnuts. Pretty and pretty good.

Puffed Pear Pancake

This is one of my favorite recipes, one of the easiest and one of the splashiest—no one will ever suspect that this dramatic, high-rising dessert is child's play to produce. Technically, it's not really a pancake because it's baked only on one side, but I don't think anyone should argue with greatness—and this pancake, laced with caramelized pears and baked to perfection in the oven, is great.

ONE 10-INCH PANCAKE, TO SERVE 2 TO 4 PEOPLE

2 cups diced peeled pears

1 tablespoon fresh lemon juice

6 tablespoons unsalted butter

¼ cup plus 2 tablespoons sugar

1 tablespoon brandy or dark rum

½ cup milk

½ cup all-purpose flour

2 large eggs

Confectioners' sugar for dusting

1. In a small bowl, toss the pears with the lemon juice. Melt 2 tablespoons of the butter in a medium skillet over medium-high heat. Add 2 tablespoons of the sugar and the pears and cook, stirring frequently, until the pears are lightly caramelized, about 7 minutes. Add the brandy and cook for a minute more. Remove the skillet from the heat and set aside.

2. Center a rack in the oven and preheat the oven to 425°F. In a medium bowl, whisk together the milk, flour, the remaining ¼ cup sugar, and the eggs until smooth. Stir in the pears.

3. Melt the remaining 4 tablespoons butter in a 10-inch ovenproof skillet, tilting the pan to coat the sides with melted butter. Pour the pear mixture into the skillet and cook over medium heat for 1 minute; do not stir. Place the skillet in the oven and bake until the pancake is puffed and golden, 12 to 15 minutes. Sprinkle with confectioners' sugar and serve immediately. If you want, after you've dusted the pancake with confectioners' sugar, you can run it under the broiler to caramelize the sugar. You'll get a nice finish but you'll lose some of the pancake's eye-popping puff.

SERVING: Make sure everyone's at the table when the pancake is ready, because it loses its puff very quickly. Cut the pancake into wedges and serve directly from the skillet. If you want, you can pass a little Spiced Apple-Pear Butter (page 39).

4

CHAPTER

Wrap-Arounds

*Savory and Sweet Filled
Crêpes and Blintzes*

A Short Note on Crêpes and Blintzes Crêpes are pancakes, but less so. Paper-thin and wrapped around anything from jam to ham, crêpes are the French version of our flapjacks. They're just as easy to make as pancakes but seem more sophisticated.

If a crêpe is less of a pancake, a blintz is more of a crêpe. Its batter is similar but slightly richer and, like crêpes, blintzes are baked in a small flat-bottomed skillet with short sides. However, unlike crêpes or pancakes, blintzes are cooked on one side only and then cooked again (sautéed, actually) once they are filled. The result is a crispy wrapper around a luscious filling. It's the Eastern European version of an egg roll, and it's swell.

Like pancakes, crêpes and blintzes can be savory or sweet and are fun to fiddle with: See what you've got in your refrigerator and turn it into a filling (that's how I created Choco-Banana Crêpes). Set your imagination to searching for interesting toppings, and don't think twice about using a crêpe filling for a blintz; they're easily interchangeable.

Savory Wheat Crêpes

In French crêperies, the menu will give you a choice of savory crêpes made with wheat flour (like these) or *galettes de sarrasin*, crêpes made with buckwheat flour, a specialty of Brittany. In either case, the crêpes will be the right wrapper for any savory filling and, if need be, the light, paper-thin crêpes can be used for sweets too. Just remember that crêpe batter needs to rest for at least an hour before you use it, so plan ahead.

TEN TO TWELVE 7 ½-INCH CRÊPES

½ cup all-purpose flour	2 tablespoons flavorless oil, such as
½ cup milk	canola
½ cup water	½ teaspoon salt
2 large eggs	Unsalted butter for cooking

1. Place all the ingredients in a blender or a food processor fitted with the metal blade and process for a few seconds, until smooth. Scrape down the sides of the container with a rubber spatula and process again for about 15 seconds, until thoroughly blended.

2. Transfer the batter to a pitcher with a pouring spout or a bowl, cover with plastic wrap, and allow to rest for an hour. (If you want to let the batter rest longer, refrigerate it for up to a day.) Don't skip this rest—the time is needed to relax the gluten in the flour.

3. Place a nonstick or seasoned 7½-inch crêpe pan over medium heat. Brush the surface with a bit of butter (I rub the pan with the end of a stick of butter) and pour in about 2 tablespoons of batter, lifting the pan from the heat as soon as the batter hits it and tilting it so that the batter forms a thin, even layer. If you have any excess batter in the pan, pour it back into the pitcher. Then, when the batter has just set, cut off the "tail" (the batter that stuck to the side of the pan when you poured the excess back) so you have a round pancake.

4. Cook the crêpe until the top is set and the underside is golden. To check the underside, you may need to run a blunt knife or thin spatula around the edge of the crêpe to loosen it. Flip the crêpe over using a spatula or your fingers (fingers work best here, but be careful, the crêpe is very hot) and cook until the underside is lightly browned. (The second side will never be as brown as the first.) Transfer the crêpe to a piece of waxed paper. Continue making the rest of the batch, stacking the finished crêpes between sheets of waxed paper.

S E R V I N G : The crêpes can be used immediately or cooled, wrapped airtight, and stored in the freezer for up to 1 month.

Savory Buckwheat Crêpes

Buckwheat crêpes, a.k.a. *galettes de sarrasin*, are a little thicker than regular wheat flour crêpes and a lot more assertive, thanks to the strong, nutlike flavor of buckwheat. Rarely used in desserts, buckwheat crêpes can be used in any savory crêpe recipe. Like all crêpe recipes, the batter needs at least an hour's rest, so remember to figure this into your schedule.

ABOUT SIXTEEN 7 ½-INCH CRÊPES

½ cup buckwheat flour

⅓ cup all-purpose flour

1 cup milk

¾ cup water

3 large eggs

2 tablespoons flavorless oil, such as
   canola

1 teaspoon salt

Unsalted butter for cooking

1. Place all the ingredients in a blender or a food processor fitted with the metal blade and process for a few seconds until smooth. Scrape down the sides of the container with a rubber spatula and process for about 15 seconds, until thoroughly blended.

2. Transfer the batter to a pitcher with a pouring spout or a bowl, cover with plastic wrap, and allow to rest for an hour. (If you want to let the batter rest longer, refrigerate it for up to a day.) Don't skip this rest—the time is needed to relax the gluten in the flour.

3. Place a nonstick or seasoned 7½-inch crêpe pan over medium heat. Brush the surface with a bit of butter (I rub the pan with the end of a stick of butter) and pour in about 2 tablespoons of batter, lifting the pan from the heat as soon as the batter hits it and tilting it so that the batter forms a thin, even layer. If you have any excess batter in the pan, pour it back into the pitcher. Then, when the batter has just set, cut off the "tail" (the batter that stuck to the side of the pan when you poured the excess back) so you have a round pancake.

4. Cook the crêpe until the top is set and the underside is golden. To check the underside, you may need to run a blunt knife or thin spatula around the edge of the crêpe to loosen it. Flip the crêpe over using a spatula or your fingers (fingers work best here, but be careful, the crêpe is very hot) and cook until the underside is lightly browned. (The second side will never be as brown as the first.) Transfer the crêpe to a piece of waxed paper. Continue making the rest of the batch, stacking the finished crêpes between sheets of waxed paper.

SERVING: The crêpes can be used immediately or cooled, wrapped airtight, and stored in the freezer for up to 1 month.

Popeyes

The first meal I had on my first trip to Paris was a "Popeye" at a little crêperie near the Pont Neuf. As you'd expect in a crêpe named for a he-man who got his strength from spinach, Le Popeye spotlighted the iron-rich vegetable. What you might not have guessed was that it also had grated Gruyère cheese and a sunny-side-up egg, came with a large bowl of hard apple cider, and cost under two dollars. For years, every time we returned to Paris, my husband and I would have a meal at the same crêperie and we'd always order the Popeye. Nowadays, prices in Paris are steeper but the combination remains winning, and one easily duplicated at home. For best results, cook the spinach and fry the eggs to almost set before warming the crêpes.

4 CRÊPES

½ cup fresh spinach, trimmed and washed (see Note)

4 large eggs

2 teaspoons (approximately) unsalted butter

4 Savory Wheat Crêpes (page 116) or Savory Buckwheat Crêpes (page 118)

1 cup grated Gruyère cheese (if necessary, substitute imported Swiss cheese)

Salt and freshly ground black pepper to taste

Unsalted butter for cooking

1. Place the spinach in a large saucepan, cover, and cook, using only the water clinging to the leaves, until wilted, about 5 minutes. Drain. When cool enough to handle, squeeze the leaves between your palms to remove excess moisture. Set aside.

2. To fry the eggs, heat a griddle or skillet until a drop of water dances on its surface. Then, if the griddle is not nonstick, butter it. Carefully crack the eggs onto the griddle so that the yolks remain intact. Cook until the whites are opaque and the yolks set just enough to hold in place when you lift the eggs; you don't want to cook the eggs completely, because they are going to be reheated. Using a wide metal spatula, lift the eggs onto a baking sheet and reserve.

3. If you're going to assemble the crêpes on a griddle, you may be able to make them all at one time. If you're using a skillet, you'll probably have to assemble the crêpes one at a time, in which case you might want to heat your oven to 200°F and keep the finished crêpes, loosely covered with foil, in the oven on a baking sheet until the whole batch is ready.

4. Lightly butter the griddle or skillet. Lay out as many crêpes as will fit on your griddle or in your pan and sprinkle a quarter of the cheese followed by a quarter of the spinach over each one. Top with a sunny-side-up egg and cook until the cheese is melted and the spinach and egg(s) are warm. Serve immediately, or keep warm in the preheated oven while you make the rest of the batch.

NOTE: Look for packaged baby spinach at your market; it doesn't need to be trimmed.

SERVING: Not surprisingly, I'm a fan of serving these with French hard cider, available in wine and spirits shops as well as some specialty markets. You can serve these as an appetizer, although your French friends may say it's not done, or make them the main course. I'd suggest getting the meal started with a soup, serving the Popeyes solo (perhaps two to a person if you've got a few hungry guests), and then following them up with a crispy salad and dessert.

Golden Oniony-Ricotta Crêpes Topped with Tomato Sauce

These are soft, oniony-sweet, seductively comforting, and just right for a light supper on a cool night. The crêpes are filled with an onion-ricotta mixture, rolled, baked, and topped with a sprinkling of Parmesan and a drizzle of a quickly made tomato sauce.

4 CRÊPES

1 tablespoon olive oil	4 Savory Wheat Crêpes (page 116) or
4 cups thinly sliced onions	Savory Buckwheat Crêpes (page 118)
1 cup part-skim ricotta	2 teaspoons unsalted butter
1 tablespoon minced fresh flat-leaf	2 tablespoons freshly grated Parmesan
parsley	cheese
1/8 teaspoon freshly grated nutmeg	
1/2 teaspoon salt, or more to taste	
1/2 teaspoon freshly ground black	Tomato Sauce with Sun-Dried Tomatoes
pepper, or more to taste	(recipe follows), warmed, for topping

1. Heat the olive oil in a large skillet, and add the onions. Cook over medium heat, stirring often, until the onions are soft and golden, about 15 to 20 minutes. Set aside.

2. Preheat the oven to 350°F. Butter a baking pan that is large enough to hold the crêpes rolled up and placed side by side (an 8-inch square pan should be right). Mix together the onions, ricotta, parsley, nutmeg, salt, and pepper.

122

3. Lay a crêpe on a work surface and spread a quarter of the filling down the center third of the crêpe. Turn the top and bottom of the crêpe over just a little bit to create a seal on either end, then fold the sides over the filling. Place the filled crêpe in the prepared pan, seam side down, and fill the remaining crêpes. Cut the butter into tiny pieces and scatter evenly over the crêpes. Cover the pan with foil and bake for 15 minutes.

4. Remove the foil and sprinkle the crêpes with the cheese. Drizzle over a small amount of Tomato Sauce (you'll have sauce left over to pass at the table). Heat in the oven just until the cheese melts and the sauce is bubbly, about 5 minutes. Serve immediately.

Tomato Sauce with Sun-Dried Tomatoes

1 cup tomato sauce, homemade or
store-bought
2 teaspoons very finely minced
sun-dried tomatoes

1 teaspoon sherry vinegar (or substitute
balsamic vinegar)
Salt and freshly ground black pepper
to taste

Place the tomato sauce and sun-dried tomatoes in a small saucepan and bring to a boil. Lower the heat and simmer for 5 minutes. Add the vinegar and simmer for another minute. Add the salt and pepper and remove from the heat. The sauce can be made up to 3 days ahead and stored in the refrigerator in a tightly covered jar; reheat before using.

SERVING: You could serve these, one to a diner, as an appetizer, or make these the main course, adding vegetables on the side and following with a grand salad.

Blintzes

Blintzes are Eastern European pancakes . . . kind of. They are thinner than American pancakes and thicker than French crêpes, but their greatest difference is the fact that they're cooked on just one side, then filled and cooked a second time. Blintzes—the name is used both for the pancakes and the filled finished product—are little envelopes, stuffed with sweet or savory mixtures and then sautéed in butter until crisp and golden. I haven't met a person who hasn't found them irresistible.

Like crêpe batter, the batter for blintzes needs to rest for at least an hour before it's used, so plan ahead. And while you're planning ahead, you might want to multiply the recipe because blintzes freeze perfectly.

A B O U T   S I X T E E N   7 ½ - I N C H   B L I N T Z E S

1 cup all-purpose flour

4 large eggs, at room temperature

1 cup milk, at room temperature

2 tablespoons unsalted butter, melted

½ teaspoon sugar

Pinch of salt

Unsalted butter for cooking

1. Place all the ingredients in a blender or a food processor fitted with the metal blade and process, stopping once or twice to scrape down the sides of the container, until smooth and well combined. Transfer the batter to a pitcher with a spout or a bowl, cover with plastic wrap, and let rest in the refrigerator for at least 1 hour. (It will keep covered in the refrigerator for up to 3 days.)

2. Place a nonstick or seasoned 7½-inch crêpe pan over medium heat. Brush the surface with a bit of butter (I rub the pan with the end of a stick of butter) and pour in 2 to 3 tablespoons of batter, lifting the pan from the heat as soon as the batter hits it and tilting it so that the batter forms a thin, even layer. If you have any excess batter in the pan, pour it back into the pitcher. Then, when the batter has just set, cut off the "tail" (the batter that stuck to the side of the pan when you poured the excess back) so you have a round pancake.

3. Cook the blintz for 1½ to 2 minutes, until tiny bubbles appear on the surface and the top looks dull. If you lift the pancake, the bottom should be firm and, perhaps, blistered; it shouldn't take on much color. Loosen an edge of the blintz with a knife or thin spatula and transfer the blintz (I use my fingers for this) to a sheet of waxed paper, uncooked side up. Cover with another sheet of waxed paper and a kitchen towel. Continue making the rest of the batch, stacking the finished blintzes between sheets of waxed paper under the towel.

SERVING: The blintzes can be used immediately or cooled, wrapped airtight, and stored in the freezer for up to 1 month.

Spring-Green Mushroom Rolls

The spring-green color in these soul-satisfying mushroom rolls comes from a blend of baby spinach, parsley, and a few sprigs of fresh rosemary. I love this filling for blintzes and have used it often with crêpes as well. I've also multiplied the recipe without a hitch when I've had a crowd.

8 BLINTZES

1 tablespoon olive oil

2 tablespoons finely chopped onion

½ pound mushrooms, cleaned, trimmed, and thinly sliced

½ pound farmer's cheese

1 large egg

1 cup cleaned and dried baby spinach (or an equal amount of trimmed regular spinach)

3 tablespoons chopped fresh parsley

1 teaspoon minced fresh rosemary or ¼ teaspoon dried

¾ teaspoon salt

½ teaspoon freshly ground black pepper

8 Blintzes (page 124)

About 2 tablespoons unsalted butter for cooking

Porcini or rosemary oil, homemade or store-bought, and Crème Fraîche (page 51) or sour cream (optional), for topping

1. Heat the olive oil in a large skillet over medium heat. Add the onions and mushrooms and cook, stirring frequently, until the onions are wilted and the mushrooms are soft. Remove the skillet from the heat and let cool slightly.

2. Place the farmer's cheese, egg, spinach, parsley, rosemary, salt, and pepper in a food processor fitted with the metal blade or in a blender. Process until the mixture is smooth and creamy, stopping to scrape down the sides of the container as needed. Add the onions and mushrooms, and any oil remaining in the skillet, and pulse just to chop the mushrooms and incorporate the ingredients. You can use the filling now, or pack it in a covered container and store it in the refrigerator for up to 3 days.

3. When ready to serve, preheat the oven to 400°F. Have ready a heatproof platter or a baking sheet.

4. Lay one blintz on a clean work surface, uncooked side up. Place a scant ¼ cup of filling down the center of the blintz and, using a rubber spatula, shape the filling into a thin rectangle, leaving at least an inch free at the top and bottom of the blintz. Fold the top and bottom over the filling, then fold over the sides to form a neat envelope; set aside seam side down. Continue until all the blintzes are filled.

5. Heat 2 teaspoons butter in a large skillet, preferably nonstick, over medium heat. Add as many blintzes, seam side down, as fit comfortably in the pan without crowding. Cook the blintzes until they are lightly browned on the bottom, then gently turn them with a wide spatula and cook until browned on the other side, adding more butter as needed. Transfer the blintzes, seam side down, to the platter or baking sheet and sauté the rest of the batch.

6. Bake the blintzes for 10 minutes, or until the filling is puffed and piping hot.

SERVING: If you're offering these as part of a brunch menu, I'd suggest you serve two to a plate; if they're a starter at lunch or dinner, a solo blintz should suffice. In either case, decorate the plate with a drizzle of infused oil (rosemary or porcini) and, if you'd like, a sprig of fresh rosemary and a dollop of sour cream or crème fraîche.

Sweet Crêpes

Sweeter and ever so slightly richer than savory wheat flour crêpes, sweet crêpes are the ones you see Parisians buying from street-side stands, slathering with preserves, often apricot jam, and eating on the run. Depending on what you spread or fill these crêpes with, they can be a quick snack or an elegant dessert. Don't forget—the batter needs to rest for at least an hour before you can use it.

TEN TO TWELVE 7 ½ -INCH CRÊPES

½ cup all-purpose flour	2 tablespoons unsalted butter, melted
¾ cup milk	2 tablespoons sugar
¼ cup water	Pinch of salt
2 large eggs	Unsalted butter for cooking

1. Place all the ingredients in a blender or a food processor fitted with the metal blade and process for a few seconds, until smooth. Scrape down the sides of the container with a rubber spatula and process for about 15 seconds, until thoroughly blended.

2. Transfer the batter to a pitcher with a pouring spout or a bowl, cover with plastic wrap, and allow to rest for an hour. (If you want to let the batter rest longer, refrigerate it.) Don't skip this rest—the time is needed to relax the gluten in the flour.

3. Place a nonstick or seasoned 7½-inch crêpe pan over medium heat. Brush the surface with a bit of butter (I rub the pan with the end of a stick of butter) and pour in about 2 tablespoons of batter, lifting the pan from the heat as soon as the batter hits it and tilting it so that the batter forms a thin, even layer. If you have any excess batter in the pan, pour it back into the pitcher. Then, when the batter has just set, cut off the "tail" (the batter that stuck to the side of the pan when you poured the excess back) so you have a round pancake.

4. Cook the crêpe until the top is set and the underside is golden. To check the underside, you may need to run a blunt knife or thin spatula around the edge of the crêpe to loosen it. Flip the crêpe over using a spatula or your fingers (fingers work best here, but be careful, the crêpe is very hot) and cook until the underside is lightly browned. (The second side will never be as brown as the first.) Transfer the crêpe to a piece of waxed paper. Continue making the rest of the batch, stacking the finished crêpes between sheets of waxed paper.

S ERVING : The crêpes can be used immediately or cooled, wrapped airtight, and stored in the freezer for up to 1 month.

Butter and Jam Crêpes

Crêpes don't get simpler or yummier than these. Butter and Jam Crêpes are just as advertised: sweet crêpes warmed in butter, spread with jam, sprinkled with sugar, and served piping hot. These are the crêpes that the French, young and old, eat out of hand as any-time-of-the-day snacks. At home, you can serve these two to a plate with a small fork and knife. The recipe is for two servings; just keep multiplying to feed your crowd.

4 CRÊPES

2 teaspoons unsalted butter

4 Sweet Crêpes (page 128)

4 rounded teaspoons best-quality jam or
Apricot-Ginger Butter (recipe follows)

Sugar for sprinkling

1. Preheat your broiler.

2. Prepare one crêpe at a time. For each crêpe, melt ½ teaspoon of the butter in a nonstick or seasoned 7½-inch crêpe pan or skillet. Put the crêpe in the pan and brush it with 1 rounded teaspoon of the jam, leaving a narrow border. Let it warm for 30 seconds, or until heated through. Fold the sides of the crêpe over—you'll have a long tube—then fold the ends over just a little bit to make a rectangular envelope. Roll the crêpe out of the pan, seam side down, onto a flameproof platter or a baking sheet.

3. When ready to serve, sprinkle each crêpe with sugar and run the platter under the broiler to caramelize the sugar. Watch carefully, and remove from the broiler as soon as the sugar is bubbly and golden. Serve immediately.

Apricot-Ginger Butter

This is the most delicious apricot butter I've ever had. The color is gorgeous and the taste is clean and true—pure apricot goodness with a spark of ginger. The recipe makes a pint, but it can be doubled if you'd like to have some available for gift giving.

2 cups coarsely chopped dried
apricots (about ½ pound),
preferably plump Turkish
apricots
1 cup fresh orange juice

½ cup water
1½ tablespoons chopped peeled fresh
ginger
2 tablespoons honey
2 tablespoons sugar, or more to taste

1. Combine the apricots, orange juice, water, and ginger in a medium saucepan. Cover tightly and simmer over medium-low heat until the liquid is reduced by half and the apricots are very tender, about 20 minutes. Stir the mixture frequently so the apricots don't stick.

2. Transfer the mixture to a food processor fitted with the metal blade and puree until smooth, scraping down the sides of the bowl as needed. Add the honey and sugar and process to blend; add more sugar if desired. Pack the butter into a jar, cover with plastic wrap, and cool to room temperature. The butter is ready to be served, or cover with a tight-fitting lid and refrigerate. Refrigerated, the butter will keep for 3 weeks.

SERVING: These crêpes are best eaten the minute they're rolled off the pan. However, if you must keep them while you're making the others, place the finished crêpe on a baking sheet, brush with a little melted butter, cover loosely with foil, and keep warm in a 200°F oven for no more than 10 minutes.

Choco-Banana Crêpes

These luscious crêpes were created out of economy. I wanted to use up things I had in my refrigerator: crêpes I'd made for a dinner party two nights earlier; chocolate pastry cream I'd used to fill eclairs; an on-the-verge-of-too-ripe banana; and the last of some chocolate sauce. The result of this little housekeeping binge was so good I now set aside time to make the components specifically for this dessert. Once the pastry cream and crêpes are made, nothing could be simpler to put together. The crêpes are folded into quarters, plumped with the cream and banana slices, and then popped into a hot oven to warm. Ten minutes later they're served with chocolate sauce, if you've got it, or ice cream.

If the instructions look long, it's because I've given you detailed directions for making good pastry cream (it takes only five minutes to make the cream).

8 CRÊPES

3 tablespoons cornstarch

1 large egg

1 large egg yolk

Pinch of salt

1 cup milk (use whole milk)

3 tablespoons sugar

1½ ounces bittersweet chocolate, finely chopped or melted

½ teaspoon pure vanilla extract

8 Sweet Crêpes (page 128)

1 to 2 ripe bananas, peeled and thinly sliced

About 2 tablespoons unsalted butter, melted

Confectioners' sugar for dusting

Dark Chocolate Sauce (page 106) or premium-quality ice cream for topping

1. Fill a large bowl with ice cubes and set it in the freezer until needed.

2. To make the pastry cream, place the cornstarch, egg, yolk, and salt in a medium bowl. Add a few tablespoons of the milk and beat with a whisk until well blended. Pour the rest of the milk into a medium heavy-bottomed saucepan, add the sugar, and cook over medium-high heat until the milk is just at the boil and the sugar has dissolved.

3. Whisking all the while, pour a little of the very hot milk into the cornstarch mixture (this will temper the eggs so they won't scramble). Return the saucepan to the heat and bring the milk to a rolling boil. Whisk the boiling milk into the bowl with the cornstarch mixture, then turn the entire contents of the bowl into the saucepan. Using a wooden spoon to stir vigorously and without stop, cook the mixture over medium-high heat until it thickens and one big bubble pops on the surface. Reduce the heat to its lowest setting and keep stirring and cooking for 20 seconds more, then immediately remove the pan from the heat. From start to finish, this process will take about 5 minutes. Have courage and use high heat, but be vigilant—cook the custard too long, and it will curdle.

4. Quickly whisk in the chocolate and vanilla, then place the pan in the ice-filled bowl. Keep stirring the cream so that it cools rapidly and evenly. Once cooled, you can use the cream immediately or pour it into a jar, cover with a piece of plastic wrap pressed against its surface, and store it in the refrigerator for up to 3 days.

5. Preheat the oven to 400°F. Butter a heatproof platter or baking sheet.

6. Fold each crêpe into quarters so that it becomes a ruffle-edged triangle with two pockets (one between the first and second layers and the other between the third and fourth), and place on the heatproof platter.

continued

7. Fill each pocket with a teaspoon of pastry cream. Peel and thinly slice the bananas; tuck 4 slices of banana into each pocket. Brush the top of each crêpe with a little butter. Heat the crêpes in the oven for 8 minutes, or until the filling is warm and a little puffed and the crêpes are slightly crispy around the edges. Immediately remove from the oven.

SERVING: Plan on one filled crêpe per diner. Using a wide metal spatula, transfer each crêpe to a dessert plate and dust generously with confectioners' sugar. To finish, drizzle Dark Chocolate Sauce around each crêpe or place a large scoop of ice cream (vanilla, chocolate, or coffee would be good) at the point of the triangle. Serve warm. If you don't have sauce or ice cream, don't let it stop you from serving these; they're fine on their own with just the dusting of sugar. They'd also be nice with a splash of heated and flamed brandy or banana liqueur.

Rum-Flavored Almond Cream Crêpes

The filling for these sweet crêpes is fragrant almond cream, the type that's used to fill the finest French fruit tarts. The recipe makes enough almond cream to fill ten to twelve crêpes, but if you're just serving a couple instead, I'd still make the entire amount—you'll be happy to have this cream stored in your freezer for the next crêpe party or ready to fill a pear tart. In this recipe, I fill the crêpes with the cream, heat them for a few minutes in a hot oven, and then, for a dramatic and delectable finish, douse them with flaming rum.

10 CRÊPES

½ cup (about 2 ounces) blanched
  almonds (whole, slivered, sliced,
  or chopped)

⅓ cup sugar

4 tablespoons (½ stick) unsalted
  butter, at room temperature

1 large egg

1 large egg yolk

¾ cup dark rum

10 Sweet Crêpes (page 128)

About 3 tablespoons unsalted butter,
  melted

Confectioners' sugar for dusting

1. To make the almond cream, place the almonds and sugar in a food processor fitted with the metal blade or in a blender and process until the almonds are pulverized and the mixture resembles flour.

2. Place the softened butter in the bowl of an electric mixer, fitted with a whisk attachment if you have it. Add a tablespoon of the almond flour and whip at high speed until the butter is very creamy and pale. Turn the machine to low and add the egg and half the remaining

135

almond flour. Beat at low to combine, then raise the speed to high and beat until well blended. Return the machine to low and add the yolk and the remaining almond flour. Mix at low until combined, then whip the mixture at high speed until thoroughly blended. Add 1 tablespoon of the dark rum and mix to blend. You can use the almond cream immediately or store it in a covered container in the refrigerator for up to 3 days.

3. Preheat the oven to 400°F. Butter a heatproof platter or baking sheet (or use a nonstick pan).

4. Fold each crêpe into quarters so that it becomes a ruffle-edged triangle with two pockets (one between the first and second layers and the other between the third and fourth), and place on the heatproof platter.

5. Fill each pocket with a teaspoon of almond cream. Brush the top of each crêpe with butter. Heat the crêpes in the oven for 8 minutes, or until the filling is warm and a little puffed and the crêpes are slightly crispy at the edges. Immediately remove from the oven.

SERVING: Use a wide metal spatula to transfer each crêpe to a dessert plate. Dust generously with confectioners' sugar. To finish, pour the remaining dark rum into a large metal ladle with a heatproof handle or a small saucepan. Heat the rum over high heat for about a minute. If you're using a ladle over a gas flame, it's likely that when the rum is hot enough (and the flames from the heat source high enough), it will self-ignite; if your rum doesn't burst into flame, carefully put a match to it. Then pour the flaming rum over the crêpes. Don't worry about extinguishing the flame—it will die out by itself when the alcohol burns off. Needless to say, this is not an operation to do under a kitchen cabinet or near a window with curtains, or when you're wearing a billowing chiffon scarf. This is, however, a technique that's easy and dramatic. If you can manage it, bring the desserts to the table still flaming. Your guests will adore it.

Cranberry Blintzes

These look and taste like a holiday, but I'd urge you to make this recipe anytime you're in the mood for a festive dish that will lift your spirits. The filling is a deeply flavored, ruby-red, made-in-minutes cranberry jam softened and smoothed with a little cream cheese and a few spoonfuls of sour cream. (It can be doubled or tripled if you're giving a party.)

6 BLINTZES

1 cup fresh or frozen cranberries

¾ cup sugar

⅓ cup plump dark or golden raisins

¼ cup fresh orange juice

½ teaspoon cinnamon

Grated zest of ½ orange

1 tablespoon orange marmalade

2 ounces cream cheese, at room
  temperature

3 tablespoons sour cream

1 large egg

6 Blintzes (page 124)

About 2 tablespoons unsalted butter
  for cooking

Confectioners' sugar for dusting

Cranberry Honey (page 20), maple syrup,
  premium-quality vanilla ice cream, or
  sour cream for topping

1. In a medium saucepan, mix together the cranberries, sugar, raisins, orange juice, cinnamon, and zest. Place the pan over medium heat and cook, stirring frequently with a wooden spoon, until the mixture boils and thickens and the spoon leaves a trail, 8 to 10 minutes. The jam should be the consistency of juicy preserves; it will thicken more as it cools. Remove the pan from the heat and add the orange marmalade. Transfer the jam to a bowl, cover with a sheet of plastic wrap pressed against the surface of the jam, and cool to room temperature. You can finish making the filling as soon as the mixture is cool or store the jam, covered, in the refrigerator for up to 3 days.

2. Place the cream cheese, sour cream, and egg in a food processor fitted with the metal blade, and process until velvety smooth. Add half of the jam and blend to a chunky puree. Transfer the mixture to a bowl and fold in the remainder of the jam. The filling can be made ahead and kept covered in the refrigerator for up to 3 days.

3. At serving, preheat the oven to 400°F and ready a heatproof platter or baking sheet.

4. Lay one blintz out on a clean work surface, uncooked side up. Place a scant ¼ cup of filling down the center of the blintz and, using a rubber spatula, shape the filling into a thin rectangle, leaving at least an inch free at the top and bottom of the blintz. Fold the top and bottom over the filling, then fold over the sides to form a neat envelope; set aside seam side down. Continue until all the blintzes are filled.

5. Heat 2 teaspoons butter in a large skillet, preferably nonstick, over medium heat. Add as many blintzes, seam side down, as fit comfortably in the pan without crowding. Cook the blintzes until they are lightly browned on the bottom, then gently turn them with a wide spatula and cook until browned on the other side, adding more butter as needed. Transfer the blintzes, seam side down, to the platter or baking sheet and sauté the rest of the batch.

6. Bake the blintzes 10 minutes, until the filling is puffed and hot. Serve immediately.

SERVING: Place the blintz(es) in the center of a dessert plate and sprinkle with confectioners' sugar. If you are serving Cranberry Honey or maple syrup, drizzle a little over each blintz and pour the remainder into a pitcher to pass at the table. If you've opted for ice cream or sour cream, just put a scoop on top of the blintz and let it melt—it's delicious that way.

Cherry-Chocolate Blintzes

This blintz was inspired by a simple Italian dessert I admired, a mixture of whipped ricotta and chunks of chocolate. Not able to resist elaborating, I've added walnuts, a bit of cinnamon, a spoonful of brandy, and lots of plump winey-tart dried cherries. Wrapped in a blintz and cooked in butter, these are top-drawer brunch fare. As always, you can double the recipe if your group is large.

10 BLINTZES

*One 15-ounce container part-skim
  or reduced-fat ricotta*

1 large egg

1 large egg yolk

*½ cup chopped walnuts, pecans,
  or almonds*

3 tablespoons sugar

1 tablespoon brandy

1 teaspoon pure vanilla extract

¼ teaspoon cinnamon (optional)

Pinch of salt

*½ cup plump dried cherries, halved
  if large*

¼ cup mini semisweet chocolate chips

10 Blintzes (page 124)

*About 2 tablespoons unsalted butter
  for cooking*

Confectioners' sugar for dusting

*Dark Chocolate Sauce (page 106) or
  honey for topping (optional)*

1. Place the ricotta, egg, yolk, nuts, sugar, brandy, vanilla, cinnamon, and salt in a food processor fitted with the metal blade or a blender. Pulse until the mixture is smooth, stopping to scrape down the sides of the container as needed. Scrape the mixture into a medium bowl. With a rubber spatula, fold in the cherries and chocolate chips. You can use the filling now or store it, well covered, in the refrigerator for up to 2 days.

2. At serving time, preheat the oven to 400°F. Have ready a heatproof platter or baking sheet.

3. Lay one blintz on a clean work surface, uncooked side up. Place a scant ¼ cup of filling down the center of the blintz and, using a rubber spatula, shape the filling into a thin rectangle, leaving at least an inch free at the top and bottom of the blintz. Fold the top and bottom over the filling, then fold over the sides to form a neat envelope. Continue until all the blintzes are filled.

4. Heat 2 teaspoons butter in a large skillet, preferably nonstick, over medium heat. Add as many blintzes, seam side down, as fit comfortably in the pan without crowding. Cook the blintzes until they are lightly browned on the bottom, then gently turn them with a wide spatula and cook until browned on the other side, adding more butter as needed. Transfer the blintzes, seam side down, to the platter or baking sheet and sauté the rest of the batch.

5. Bake the blintzes for about 8 minutes, until the filling is puffed and piping hot. Serve immediately.

S E R V I N G : When the blintzes are heated through, the filling will be very hot, aromatic, and, when cut, smooth and creamy enough to be both filling and sauce. Therefore, I usually serve these dressed with nothing more than a dusting of confectioners' sugar. Depending on the time of day and what part of the meal the blintzes are starring in, you might consider passing a pitcher of Dark Chocolate Sauce or drizzling a little honey around the side of the plate.

Index

143

144

P